THE FORCE OF NONVIOLENCE

THE FORCE OF NONVIOLENCE

An Ethico-Political Bind

Judith Butler

VERSO
London • New York

First published by Verso 2020
© Judith Butler 2020

The moral rights of the author have been asserted

13 5 7 9 10 8 6 4 2

Verso
UK: 6 Meard Street, London W1F 0EG
US: 20 Jay Street, Suite 1010, Brooklyn, NY 11201
versobooks.com

Verso is the imprint of New Left Books

ISBN-13: 978-1-78873-276-5
ISBN-13: 978-1-78873-278-9 (UK EBK)
ISBN-13: 978-1-78873-279-6 (US EBK)

British Library Cataloguing in Publication Data
A catalogue record for this book is available from the British Library

Library of Congress Cataloging-in-Publication Data
Names: Butler, Judith, 1956- author.
Title: The force of nonviolence : an ethico-political bind / Judith
   Butler.
Description: Brooklyn : Verso Books, 2020. | Includes index. | Summary:
   "Situating non-violence at the cross-roads of the ethical and political, The Force of Non-Violence brings into focus the ethical binds that emerge within the force field of violence. Non-violence is very often misunderstood as a passive practice that emanates from a calm region of the soul, or as an individualist ethic with an unrealistic relation to existing forms of power. This book argues for an aggressive form of non-violence that struggles with psychic ambivalence and seeks to embody social ideals of inter-dependency and equality. Only through a critique of individualism can the ethical and political ideal of non-violence be understood in relation to the ideal of equality and the demand for grievability. In this psychosocial and philosophical reflection that draws upon Foucault, Fanon, Freud, and Benjamin, Butler argues that to oppose violence now requires understanding its different modalities, including the regulation of the grievability of lives. The book shows how "racial and demographic phantasms" enter into the rationale for inflicting state violence and other modes of "letting die" by investing violence in those who are most severely exposed to its effects and subjugated to its lethal power. The struggle for non-violence is found in modes of resistance and movements for social transformation that separate off aggression from its destructive aims to affirm the living potentials of radical egalitarian politics"-- Provided by publisher.
Identifiers: LCCN 2019038460 (print) | LCCN 2019038461 (ebook) | ISBN
   9781788732765 (hardback) | ISBN 9781788732796 (ebook)
Subjects: LCSH: Nonviolence--Moral and ethical aspects. | Nonviolence. |
   Individualism.
Classification: LCC BJ1459.5 .B88 2020 (print) | LCC BJ1459.5 (ebook) |
   DDC 179.7--dc23
LC record available at https://lccn.loc.gov/2019038460
LC ebook record available at https://lccn.loc.gov/2019038461

Typeset in Adobe Garamond by Hewer Text UK Ltd, Edinburgh
Printed and bound by CPI Group (UK) Ltd, Croydon CR0 4YY

Whenever and to whatever extent there is room for the use of arms or physical force or brute force, there and to that extent is there so much less possibility for soul force.

Mahatma Gandhi

The choice today is no longer between violence and nonviolence. It is either nonviolence or nonexistence.

Martin Luther King, Jr.

The legacy (of nonviolence) is not that of an individual legacy but a collective legacy of vast people who stood together in unity to proclaim that they would never surrender to forces of racism and inequality.

Angela Davis

Contents

Acknowledgments

I am thankful to audiences and respondents who heard earlier versions of these chapters as the Tanner Lectures at Yale University in 2016, the Gifford Lectures at the University of Glasgow in 2018, and the Cuming Lectures at University College Dublin in 2019. I thank, as well, audiences and colleagues for their critical engagement at the Centre de Cultura Contemporània de Barcelona, University of Zurich, Sciences Po in Paris, Meiji University in Tokyo, the Free University of Amsterdam, the Institute for Philosophy and Social Theory at the University of Belgrade, the Institute for Critical Social Inquiry at the New School for Social Research, WISER at the University of the Witwatersrand, the Psychology and the Other conference in Cambridge in 2015, and the Modern Language Association meetings in 2014. I am most thankful to my students at the University of California, Berkeley, and my colleagues in the International Consortium of Critical Theory Programs, who have kept my mind sharper than it otherwise would have been. As always, I thank Wendy Brown for the joyful company of her intelligence, and for her enduring support. I dedicate this book to a friend and colleague precious to the UC Berkeley community, Saba Mahmood. Of course, she would have disagreed with my argument here, and I would have treasured that exchange.

Chapters 2 and 3 are revised and expanded versions of the Tanner Lectures delivered in 2016 at Yale University's Whitney Humanities Center. Chapter 4 appeared in earlier form in Richard G. T. Gipps and Michael Lacewing, eds., *The Oxford Handbook of Philosophy and Psychoanalysis*, Oxford: Oxford University Press, 2019.

Introduction

The case for nonviolence encounters skeptical responses from across the political spectrum. There are those on the left who claim that violence alone has the power to effect radical social and economic transformation, and others who claim, more modestly, that violence should remain one of the tactics at our disposal to bring about such change. One can put forth arguments in favor of nonviolence or, alternately, the instrumental or strategic use of violence, but those arguments can only be conducted in public if there is general agreement on what constitutes violence and nonviolence. One major challenge faced by those in favor of nonviolence is that "violence" and "nonviolence" are disputed terms. For instance, some people call wounding acts of speech "violence," whereas others claim that language, except in the case of explicit threats, cannot properly be called "violent." Yet others hold to restrictive views of violence, understanding the "blow" as its defining physical moment; others insist that economic and legal structures are "violent," that they act upon bodies, even if they do not always take the form of physical violence. Indeed, the figure of the blow has tacitly organized some of the major debates on violence, suggesting that violence is something that happens between two parties in a heated encounter. Without disputing the violence of the physical blow, we can nevertheless insist that social structures or systems, including systemic racism, are violent. Indeed, sometimes the physical strike to the head or the body is an expression of systemic violence, at which point one has to be able to understand the relationship of act to structure, or system. To understand structural or systemic violence, one needs to move beyond positive accounts that limit our understanding of how violence works. And one needs to find frameworks more encompassing than those that rely on two figures, one striking and the other struck. Of course, any account of violence that cannot explain the strike, the blow, the act of sexual violence (including rape), or that fails to understand the way violence can work in the intimate dyad or the face-to-face encounter, fails descriptively, and analytically, to clarify what violence is—that is, what we are talking about when we debate over violence and nonviolence.[1]

It seems like it should be easy to simply oppose violence and allow such a statement to summarize one's position on the matter. But in public debates, we see that "violence" is labile, its semantics appropriated in ways that call to be contested. States and institutions sometimes call "violent" any number of expressions of political dissent, or of opposition to the state or the authority of the institution in question. Demonstrations, encampments, assemblies, boy-cotts,

---

1   See "The Political Scope of Non-Violence," in Thomas Merton, ed., *Gandhi: On Non-Violence*, New York: New Directions, 1965, 65–78.

and strikes are all subject to being called "violent" even when they do not seek recourse to physical fighting, or to the forms of systemic or structural violence mentioned above.[2] When states or institutions do this, they seek to rename nonviolent practices as violent, conducting a political war, as it were, at the level of public semantics. If a demonstration in support of freedom of expression, a demonstration that exercises that very freedom, is called "violent," that can only be because the power that misuses language that way seeks to secure its own monopoly on violence through maligning the opposition, justifying the use of police, army, or security forces against those who seek to exercise and defend freedom in that way. American studies scholar Chandan Reddy has argued that the form taken by liberal modernity in the United States posits the state as a guarantee of a freedom from violence that fundamentally depends on unleashing violence against racial minorities, and against all peoples characterized as irrational and outside the national norm.[3] The state, in his view, is founded in racial violence and continues to inflict it against minorities in systematic ways. Thus, racial violence is understood to serve the state's self-defense. How often in the United States and elsewhere are black and brown people on the street or in their homes called or deemed "violent" by police who arrest them or gun them down, even when they are unarmed, even when they are walking or running away, when they are trying to make

---

2 For an overview of nonviolent actions, see Gene Sharp, *How Nonviolent Struggle Works*, Boston: The Albert Einstein Institution, 2013.

3 Chandan Reddy, *Freedom with Violence: Race, Sexuality, and the US State*, Durham, NC: Duke University Press, 2011.

a complaint themselves, or simply fast asleep?[4] It is both curious and appalling to see how the defense of violence works under such conditions, for the target has to be figured as a threat, a vessel of real or actual violence, in order for lethal police action to appear as self-defense. If the person was not doing anything demonstrably violent, then perhaps the person is simply figured as violent, as a violent *kind* of person, or as pure violence embodied in and by that person. The latter claim manifests racism more often than not.

What starts, then, as an apparently moral argument about whether to be for or against violence quickly turns into a debate about how violence is defined and who is called "violent"—and for what purposes. When a group assembles to oppose censorship or the lack of democratic freedoms, and the group is called a "mob," or is understood as a chaotic or destructive threat to the social order, then the group is both named and figured as potentially or actually violent, at which point the state can issue a justification to defend society against this violent threat. When what follows is imprisonment, injury, or killing, the violence in the scene emerges as state violence. We can name state violence as "violent" even though it has used its own power to name and to represent the dissenting power of some group of people as "violent." Similarly, a peaceful demonstration such as that which took place in Gezi Park in Istanbul in 2013,[5] or a letter calling for peace such as the one signed by many Turkish

---

4 For statistics on "justifiable" police homicides of African Americans, see "Black Lives Matter: Race, Policing, and Protest," Wellesley Research Guides, libguides.wellesley.edu/blacklivesmatter/statistics.

5 See "Gezi Park Protests 2013: Overview," University of Pennsylvania Libraries Guides, guides.library.upenn.edu/Gezi_Park.

scholars in 2016,[6] can be effectively figured and represented as a "violent" act only if the state either has its own media or exercises sufficient control over the media. Under such conditions, exercising rights of assembly is called a manifestation of "terrorism," which, in turn, calls down the state censor, clubbing and spraying by the police, termination of employment, indefinite detention, imprisonment, and exile.

As much as it would make matters easier to be able to identify violence in a way that is clear and commands consensus, this proves impossible to do in a political situation where the power to attribute violence to the opposition itself becomes an instrument by which to enhance state power, to discredit the aims of the opposition, or even to justify their radical disenfranchisement, imprisonment, and murder. At such moments, the attribution has to be countered on the grounds that it is untrue and unfair. But how is that to be done in a public sphere where semantic confusion has been sown about what is and is not violent? Are we left with a confusing array of opinions about violence and nonviolence and forced to admit to a generalized relativism? Or can we establish a way of distinguishing between a tactical attribution of violence that falsifies and inverts its direction, and those forms of violence, often structural and systemic, that too often elude direct naming and apprehension?

If one wants to make an argument in favor of nonviolence, it will be necessary to understand and evaluate the ways that violence is figured and attributed within a field

---

6 See "Academics for Peace," Frontline Defenders official website, frontlinedefenders.org.

of discursive, social, and state power; the inversions that are tactically performed; and the phantasmatic character of the attribution itself. Further, we will have to undertake a critique of the schemes by which state violence justifies itself, and the relation of those justificatory schemes to the effort to maintain its monopoly on violence. That monopoly depends upon a naming practice, one that often dissimulates violence as legal coercion or externalizes its own violence onto its target, rediscovering it as the violence of the other.

To argue for or against nonviolence requires that we establish the difference between violence and nonviolence, if we can. But there is no quick way to arrive at a stable semantic distinction between the two when that distinction is so often exploited for the purposes of concealing and extending violent aims and practices. In other words, we cannot race to the phenomenon itself without passing through the conceptual schemes that dispose the use of the term in various directions, and without an analysis of how those dispositions work. If those accused of doing violence while engaging in no violent acts seek to dispute the status of the accusation as unjustifiable, they will have to demonstrate how the allegation of violence is used—not just "what it says," but "what it is doing with what is said." Within what episteme does it gather credibility? In other words, why is it sometimes believed, and most crucially, what can be done to expose and defeat the effective character of the speech act—its plausibility effect?

To start down such a path, we have to accept that "violence" and "nonviolence" are used variably and perversely, without pitching into a form of nihilism suffused by the belief that violence and nonviolence are whatever those in power decide they should be. Part of the task of this book is to accept the difficulty of finding and securing the definition of violence when it is subject to instrumental definitions that serve political interests and sometimes state violence itself. In my view, that difficulty does not imply a chaotic relativism that would undermine the task of critical thought in order to expose an instrumental use of that distinction that is both false and harmful. Both violence and nonviolence arrive in the fields of moral debate and political analysis already inter-preted, worked over by prior usages. There is no way to avoid the demand to interpret both violence and nonviolence, and to assess the distinction between them, if we hope to oppose state violence and to reflect carefully on the justifiability of violent tactics on the left. As we wade into moral philosophy here, we find ourselves in the crosscurrents where moral and political philosophy meet, with consequences for both how we end up doing politics, and what world we seek to help bring into being.

One of the most popular arguments on the left to defend the tactical use of violence begins with the claim that many people already live in the force field of violence. Because violence is already happening, the argument continues, there is no real choice about whether or not to enter into violence through one's action: we are already inside the field of violence. According to that view, the distance that moral deliberation takes on the question of whether or not to act in a violent way is a privilege and luxury, betraying some-thing about the power of its own location. In that view, the consideration of violent action is not a choice, since one is already—and unwillingly—within the force field of violence. Because violence is happening all the time (and it is happen-ing regularly to minorities), such resistance is but a form of counter-violence.[7] Apart from a general and traditional left claim about the necessity of a "violent struggle" for revolutionary purposes, there are more specific justificatory strategies at work: violence is happening against us, so we are justified in taking violent action against those who (a) started the violence and (b) directed it against us. We do this in the name of our own lives and our right to persist in the world.

As for the claim that resistance to violence is counter-violence, we might still pose a set of questions: Even if violence is circulating all the time and we find ourselves in a force field of violence, do we want to have a say about whether violence continues to circulate? If it circulates all the time, is it therefore inevitable that it circulates? What would it mean to dispute the inevitability of its circulation? The argument may be, "Others do it, and so should we"; or else, "Others do it against us, so we should do it against them, in the name of self-preservation." These are each different, but important claims. The first holds to a principle of straightforward reciprocity, suggesting that whatever actions the other takes, I am licensed to take as well. That line of argumentation, however, sidesteps the question of whether what the other does is justifiable. The second claim links violence with self-defense and self-preservation, an argument we will take up in the subsequent chapters. For the moment, though, let us ask: Who is this "self" defended in the name of self-defense?[8] How is that self delineated from other selves, from

---

7   For a full discussion of resistance, including its paradoxical formulations, see Howard Caygill, *On Resistance: A Philosophy of Defiance*, New York: Bloomsbury, 2013.

8   Elsa Dorlin, *Se défendre: Une philosophie de la violence*, Paris: La Découverte, 2017.

history, land, or other defining relations? Is the one to whom violence is done not also in some sense part of the "self" who defends itself through an act of violence? There is a sense in which violence done to another is at once a violence done to the self, but only if the relation between them defines them both quite fundamentally.

This last proposition indicates a central concern of this book. For if the one who practices nonviolence is related to the one against whom violence is contemplated, then there appears to be a prior social relation between them; they are part of one another, or one self is implicated in another self. Nonviolence would, then, be a way of acknowledging that social relation, however fraught it may be, and of affirming the normative aspirations that follow from that prior social relatedness. As a result, an ethics of nonviolence cannot be predicated on individualism, and it must take the lead in waging a critique of individualism as the basis of ethics and politics alike. An ethics and politics of nonviolence would have to account for this way that selves are implicated in each other's lives, bound by a set of relations that can be as destructive as they can be sustaining. The relations that bind and define extend beyond the dyadic human encounter, which is why nonviolence pertains not only to human relations, but to all living and inter-constitutive relations.

To launch this inquiry into social relations, however, we would have to know what kind of potential or actual social bond holds between both subjects in a violent encounter. If the self is constituted through its relations with others, then part of what it means to preserve or negate a self is to preserve or negate the extended social ties that define the self and its world. Over and against the idea that the self will be bound to act violently in the name of its individual self-preservation, this inquiry supposes that nonviolence requires a critique of egological ethics as well as of the political legacy of individualism in order to open up the idea of selfhood as a fraught field of social relationality. That relationality is, of course, defined in part by negativity, that is, by conflict, anger, and aggression. The destructive potential of human relations does not deny all relationality, and relational perspectives cannot evade the persistence of this potential or actual destruction of social ties. As a result, relationality is not by itself a good thing, a sign of connectedness, an ethical norm to be posited over and against destruction: rather, relationality is a vexed and ambivalent field in which the question of ethical obligation has to be worked out in light of a persistent and constitutive destructive potential. Whatever "doing the right thing" turns out to be, it depends on passing through the division or struggle that conditions that ethical decision to begin with. That task is never exclusively reflexive, that is, dependent on my relation to myself alone. Indeed, when the world presents as a force field of violence, the task of nonviolence is to find ways of living and acting in that world such that violence is checked or ameliorated, or its direction turned, precisely at moments when it seems to saturate that world and offer no way out. The body can be the vector of that turn, but so too can discourse, collective practices, infrastructures, and institutions. In response to the objection that a position in favor of nonviolence is simply unrealistic, this argument maintains that nonviolence requires a critique of what counts as reality, and it affirms the power and necessity of counter-realism in times like these. Perhaps nonviolence requires a certain leave-taking from reality as it is currently constituted, laying open the possibilities that belong to a newer political imaginary.

Many on the left argue that they believe in nonviolence but make an exception for self-defense. To understand their claim, we would need to know who the "self" is—its territorial limits and boundaries, its constitutive ties. If the self that I defend is me, my relatives, others who belong to my community, nation, or religion, or those who share a language with me, then I am a closet communitarian who will, it seems, preserve the lives of those who are like me, but certainly not those who are unlike me. Moreover, I apparently live in a world in which that "self" is recognizable as a self. Once we see that certain selves are considered worth defending while others are not, is there not a problem of inequality that follows from the justification of violence in the service of self-defense? One cannot explain this form of inequality, which accords measures of grievability to groups across the global spectrum, without taking account of the racial schemes that make such grotesque distinctions between which lives are valuable (and potentially grievable, if lost) and those which are not.

Given that self-defense is very often regarded as the justifiable exception to the norms guiding a nonviolent practice, we have to consider both (a) who counts as such a self and (b) how encompassing is the "self" of self-defense (again, does it include one's family, community, religion, nation, traditional land, customary practices?). For lives not considered grievable (those treated as if they can be neither lost nor mourned), dwelling already in what Frantz Fanon called "the zone of non-being," the assertion of a life that matters, as we see in the Black Lives Matter movement, can break through the schema. Lives matter in the sense that they assume physical form within the sphere of appearance; lives matter because they are to be valued equally. And yet, the claim of self-defense on the part of those who wield power is too often a defense of power, of its prerogatives, and of the inequalities it presupposes and produces. The "self" who is defended in such cases is one who identifies with others who belong to whiteness, to a specific nation, to a party in a border dispute; and so the terms of self-defense augment the purposes of war. Such a "self" can function as a kind of regime, including as part of its extended self all those who bear similitude to one's color, class, and privilege, thus expelling from the regime of the subject/self all those marked by difference within that economy. Although we think of self-defense as a response to a blow initiated from the outside, the privileged self requires no such instigation to draw its boundaries and police its exclusions. "Any possible threat"—that is, any imagined threat, any phantasm of threat—is enough to unleash its self-entitled violence. As the philosopher Elsa Dorlin has pointed out, only some selves are regarded as entitled to self-defense.[9] Whose claims of self-defense, for instance, are more readily believed in a court of law, and whose are more likely to be discounted and dismissed? Who, in other words, bears a self that is regarded as defensible, an existence that can appear within the legal frames of power as a life worthy, worth defending, not worth losing?

One of the strongest arguments for the use of violence on the left is that it is tactically necessary in order to defeat structural or systemic violence, or to dismantle a violent

---

9   Ibid.

regime, such as apartheid, dictatorship, or totalitarianism.[10] That may well be right, and I don't dispute it. But for that argument to work, we would need to know what distinguishes the violence of the regime from the violence that seeks to take it down. Is it always possible to make that distinction? Is it sometimes necessary to suffer the fact that the distinction between the one violence and the other can collapse? In other words, does violence care about that distinction, or for that matter, any of our typologies? Does the use of violence reduplicate violence, and in directions that cannot always be restrained in advance?

Sometimes the argument in favor of violence is that it is only a means to achieve another goal. So one question is: Can violence remain a mere instrument or means for taking down violence—its structures, its regime—without becoming an end in itself? The instrumentalist defense of violence depends quite crucially on being able to show that violence can be restricted to the status of a tool, a means, without becoming an end itself. The use of the tool to realize such purposes presupposes that the tool is guided by a clear intention and remains so guided throughout the course of the action. It also depends on knowing when the course of a violent action will come to an end. What happens if

---

10   See Friedrich Engels, *Anti-Dühring*, Moscow: Progress Publishers, 1947; Étienne Balibar, "Reflections on Gewalt," *Historical Materialism* 17:1, 2009; Yves Winter, "Debating Violence on the Desert Island: Engels, Dühring and Robinson Crusoe," *Contemporary Political Theory* 13:4, 2014; Nick Hewlett, "Marx, Engels, and the Ethics of Violence in Revolt," *The European Legacy: Toward New Paradigms* 17:7, 2012, and *Blood and Progress: Violence in Pursuit of Emancipation*, Edinburgh: Edinburgh University Press, 2016.

violence gets out of hand, if it is used for purposes for which it was never intended, exceeding and defying its governing intention? What if violence is precisely the kind of phenomenon that is constantly "getting out of hand"? Lastly, what if the use of violence as a means to achieve a goal licenses, implicitly or effectively, the use of violence more broadly, thereby bringing more violence into the world? Does that not lead to the possibility of a situation in which others with contrary intentions rely upon that revitalized license in order to realize their own intentions, to pursue destructive aims that are contrary to the ends constrained by its instrumental use—aims that may not be governed by any clear intention at all, or may prove to be destructive, unfocused, and unintentional?[11]

We can see that at the outset of any discussion about violence and nonviolence, we are caught up in another set of issues. First, the fact that "violence" is used strategically to describe situations that are interpreted very differently suggests that *violence is always interpreted.* That thesis does not mean that violence is nothing but an interpretation, where interpretation is conceived as a subjective and arbitrary mode of designation. Rather, violence is interpreted in the sense that it appears within frameworks that are sometimes incommensurable or conflicting, and so it appears differently—or altogether fails to appear—depending on how it is worked over by the framework(s) at issue. Stabilizing a definition of violence depends less on an enumeration of its instances than

_____

11   For a contrasting view, see scott crow, ed., *Setting Sights: Histories and Reflections on Community Armed Self-Defense*, Oakland: PM Press, 2018.

on a conceptualization that can take account of its oscillations within conflicting political frameworks. Indeed, the construction of a new framework tasked with such a purpose is one of the aims of this project.

Second, nonviolence is very often understood to be a moral position, a matter of individual conscience or of the reasons given for an individual choice not to engage in a violent way. It may be, however, that the most persuasive reasons for the practice of nonviolence directly imply a critique of individualism and require that we rethink the social bonds that constitute us as living creatures. It is not simply that an individual abrogates his or her conscience or deeply held principles in acting violently, but that certain "ties" required for social life, that is, the life of a social creature, are imperiled by violence. Similarly, the argument that justifies violence on the basis of self-defense appears to know in advance what that "self" is, who has the right to have one, and where its boundaries lie. If the "self" is conceived as relational, however, then the defenders of self-defense must give a good account of what bounds that self. If one self is vitally connected to a set of others and cannot be conceived without them, then when and where does that singular self start and end? The argument against violence, then, not only implies a critique of individualism, but an elaboration of those social bonds or relations that require nonviolence. Nonviolence as a matter of individual morality thus gives way to a social philosophy of living and sustainable bonds.

Moreover, the account of requisite social bonds has to be thought in relation to the socially unequal ways that "selves" worth defending are articulated within a political field.[12] The description of social bonds without which life is imperiled takes place at the level of a social ontology, to be understood more as a social imaginary than as a metaphysics of the social. In other words, we can assert in a general way that social interdependency characterizes life, and then proceed to account for violence as an attack on that interdependency, an attack on persons, yes; but perhaps most fundamentally, it is an attack on "bonds." And yet, interdependency, though accounting for differentials of independence and dependence, implies social equality: each is dependent, or formed and sustained in relations of depending upon, and being depended upon. What each depends upon, and what depends upon each one, is varied, since it is not just other human lives, but other sensate creatures, environments, and infrastructures: we depend upon them, and they depend on us, in turn, to sustain a livable world. To refer to equality in such a context is not to speak of an equality among all persons, if by "person" we mean a singular and distinct individual, gaining its definition by its boundary. Singularity and distinctness exist, as do boundaries, but they constitute differentiating characteristics of beings who are defined and sustained by virtue of their interrelationality. Without that overarching sense of the interrelational, we take the bodily boundary to be the end rather than the threshold of the person, the site of passage and porosity, the evidence of an openness to alterity that is definitional of the body itself. The threshold of the body, the body as threshold, undermines the idea of the body as a unit. Thus equality cannot be reduced to a calculus that accords each abstract person the same value,

---

12   Dorlin, *Se défendre*, 41–64.

since the equality of persons has now to be thought precisely in terms of social interdependency. So, though it is true that each person should be treated equally, equal treatment is not possible outside of a social organization of life in which material resources, food distribution, housing, work, and infrastructure seek to achieve equal conditions of livability. Reference to such equal conditions of livability is therefore essential to the determination of "equality" in any substantive sense of the term.

Further, when we ask whose lives count as "selves" worth defending, that is, eligible for self-defense, the question only makes sense if we recognize pervasive forms of inequality that establish some lives as disproportionately more livable and grievable than others. They establish this inequality within a particular framework, but this inequality is historical and contested by competing frameworks. It says nothing about the intrinsic value of any life. Further, as we think about the prevailing and differential ways that populations are valued and disvalued, protected and abandoned, we come up against forms of power that establish the unequal worth of lives by establishing their unequal grievability. And here, I do not mean to treat "populations" as a sociological given, since they are to some degree produced by their common exposure to injury and destruction, the differential ways they are regarded as grievable (and worth sustaining) and ungrievable (already lost and, hence, easy to destroy or to expose to forces of destruction).

The discussion of social bonds and the demographics of unequal grievability may seem unrelated to the opening discussion of the arguments used to justify violence or to defend nonviolence. The point, however, is that all these arguments presuppose ideas about what counts as violence, since violence is always interpreted in such discussion. They

presuppose as well views on individualism and on social relationality, interdependency, demographics, and equality. If
we ask what violence destroys, or what grounds we have for
naming and opposing violence in the name of nonviolence,
then we have to situate violent practices (as well as institutions, structures, and systems) in light of the conditions of
life that they destroy. Without an understanding of the conditions of life and livability, and their relative difference, we can
know neither what violence destroys nor why we should care.

Third, as Walter Benjamin made clear in his 1920 essay
"Critique of Violence," an instrumentalist logic has governed
the prevailing ways in which violence has been justified.[13]
One of the first questions he poses in that complex essay is:
Why has the instrumentalist framework been accepted as the
necessary one for thinking about violence? Instead of asking
what ends violence can achieve, why not turn the question
back on itself and ask: What justifies the instrumentalist
framework for debating the justifiability of violence, a framework, in other words, that relies on the means/ends distinction? In fact, Benjamin's point proves to be slightly different:
If we only think about violence within the framework of its
possible justification or lack of justification, does that framework not determine the phenomenon of violence in advance?
Not only does Benjamin's analysis alert us to the ways that
the instrumentalist framework determines the phenomenon, but it leads to the following question: *Can violence and*

---

13   Walter Benjamin, "Critique of Violence," in Marcus Bullock and
Michael Jennings, eds., *Walter Benjamin: Selected Writings, Volume 1: 1913–
1926*, Cambridge, MA: Harvard University Press, 2004; Walter Benjamin, *Zur
Kritik der Gewalt und Andera Aufsätze*, Frankfurt: Edition Suhrkamp, 1965.

*nonviolence both be thought beyond the instrumentalist frame-
work, and what new possibilities for ethical and political critical
thought result from that opening?*

Benjamin's text arouses anxiety among many readers
precisely because they do not want to suspend the question of what does, and does not, justify violence. The fear, it
seems, is that if we set the question of justification aside, then
all violence will be justified. That conclusion, however, by
returning the problem to the scheme of justification, fails to
understand what potential is opened up by calling into question the instrumentalist logic. Although Benjamin does not
provide the kinds of answers required for a reflection such as
this, his questioning of the means/ends framework allows us
to consider the debate outside of the terms of *technē*. For those
who claim that violence is only a provisional tactic or tool,
one challenge to their position takes this form: if tools can use
their users, and violence is a tool, then does it not follow that
violence can make use of its user? Violence as a tool is already
operating in the world before anyone takes it up: that fact
alone neither justifies nor discounts the use of the tool. What
seems most important, however, is that the tool is already
part of a practice, presupposing a world conducive to its use;
that the use of the tool builds or rebuilds a specific kind of
world, activating a sedimented legacy of use.[14] When any of
us commit acts of violence, we are, in and through those acts,
building a more violent world. What might at first seem to
be merely an instrument, a technē, to be discarded when its
goal is accomplished turns out to be a praxis: a means that

---

14   See my "Protest, Violent, Nonviolent," *Public Books*, October 13,
2017, publicbooks.org.

posits an end at the moment it is actualized, that is, where the means presupposes and enacts the end in the course of its actualization. This is a process that cannot be grasped within the instrumentalist framework. Quite apart from assiduous efforts to restrict the use of violence as means rather than an end, the actualization of violence as a means can inadvertently become its own end, producing new violence, producing violence anew, reiterating the license, and licensing further violence. Violence does not exhaust itself in the realization of a just end; rather, it renews itself in directions that exceed both deliberate intention and instrumental schemes. In other words, by acting as if the use of violence can be a means to achieve a nonviolent end, one imagines that the practice of violence does not in the act posit violence as its own end. The technē is undermined by the praxis, and the use of violence only makes the world into a more violent place, by bringing more violence into the world. Jacques Derrida's reading of Benjamin focuses on the way that justice exceeds the law.[15] But might divine violence open up the possibility of techniques of governance that exceed the law, therefore arousing interpretive debate about what qualifies as a justification, and how the framework for justification partially determines what we call "violence"? We will consider this question in Chapter 3, "The Ethics and Politics of Nonviolence."

In the course of this work, I hope to challenge some major presuppositions of nonviolence. First, nonviolence has now to be understood less as a moral position adopted

15   Jacques Derrida, "Force of Law: The 'Mystical Foundation of Authority'," in *Acts of Religion*, ed. Gil Anidjar, New York: Routledge, 2010.

by individuals in relation to a field of possible action than as a social and political practice undertaken in concert, culminating in a form of resistance to systemic forms of destruction coupled with a commitment to world building that honors global interdependency of the kind that embodies ideals of economic, social, and political freedom and equality. Second, nonviolence does not necessarily emerge from a pacific or calm part of the soul. Very often it is an expression of rage, indignation, and aggression.[16] Although some people confuse aggression with violence, it is central to the argument of this book to foreground the fact that nonviolent forms of resistance can and must be aggressively pursued. A practice of aggressive nonviolence is, therefore, not a contradiction in terms. Mahatma Gandhi insisted that *satyagraha*, or "soul force," his name for a practice and politics of nonviolence, is a nonviolent force, one that consists at once of an "insistence on truth . . . that arms the votary with matchless power." To understand this force or strength, there

---

16 See Mahatma Gandhi's defense of the nonviolence of the Satyagraha Movement before the Disorders Inquiry Committee in 1920, two years prior to his imprisonment: "Satyagraha differs from passive resistance as North Pole to South. The latter has been conceived as a weapon of the weak and does not exclude the use of physical force or violence for the purpose of gaining one's end, whereas the former has been conceived as a weapon of the strongest and excludes the use of violence in any shape or form," in Mahatma Gandhi, *Selected Political Writings*, ed. Dennis Dalton, Hackett Publishing, 1996, 6. See also Martin Luther King, Jr., "Stride Toward Freedom" where nonviolence is described as a "method," "a weapon," and a mode of "resistance" that relies on an enduring faith in the future. Influenced by Gandhi, King also drew inspiration from Thoreau's "Civil Disobedience." See also Leela Fernandes, "Beyond Retribution: The Transformative Possibilities of Nonviolence" in *Transforming Feminist Practice*, San Francisco, CA: Aunt Lute Press, 2003.

can be no simple reduction to physical strength. At the same time, "soul force" takes an embodied form. The practice of "going limp" before political power is, on the one hand, a passive posture, and is thought to belong to the tradition of passive resistance; at the same time, it is a deliberate way of exposing the body to police power, of entering the field of violence, and of exercising an adamant and embodied form of political agency. It requires suffering, yes, but for the purposes of transforming both oneself and social reality. Third, nonviolence is an ideal that cannot always be fully honored in the practice. To the degree that those who practice nonviolent resistance put their body in the way of an external power, they make physical contact, presenting a force against force in the process. Nonviolence does not imply the absence of force or of aggression. It is, as it were, an ethical stylization of embodiment, replete with gestures and modes of non-action, ways of becoming an obstacle, of using the solidity of the body and its proprioceptive object field to block or derail a further exercise of violence. When, for instance, bodies form a human barrier, we can ask whether they are blocking force or engaging in force.[17] Here, again, we are obligated to think carefully about the direction of force, and to seek to make operative a distinction between bodily force and violence. Sometimes, it may seem that obstruction *is* violence—we do, after all, speak about violent obstruction—so one question that will be

17   See Başak Ertür, "Barricades: Resources and Residues of Resistance," in Judith Butler, Zeynep Gambetti, and Leticia Sabsay, eds., *Vulnerability in Resistance*, Durham, NC: Duke University Press, 2016, 97–121; see also Banu Bargu, "The Silent Exception: Hunger Striking and Lip-Sewing," *Law, Culture, and the Humanities*, May 2017.

important to consider is whether bodily acts of resistance
involve a mindfulness of the tipping point, the site where
the force of resistance can become the violent act or practice
that commits a fresh injustice. The possibility for this kind
of ambiguity should not dissuade us of the value of this kind
of practice. Fourth, there is no practice of nonviolence that
does not negotiate fundamental ethical and political ambi-
guities, which means that "nonviolence" is not an absolute
principle, but the name of an ongoing struggle.

If nonviolence seems like a "weak" position, we should
ask: What counts as strength? How often do we see that
strength is equated with the exercise of violence or the indication of a willingness to use violence? If there is a strength
in nonviolence that emerges from this putative "weakness,"
it may be related to the powers of the weak, which include
the social and political power to establish existence for those
who have been conceptually nullified, to achieve grievability
and value for those who have been cast as dispensable, and to
insist on the possibility of both judgment and justice within
the terms of contemporary media and public policy that
offer a bewildering and sometimes quite tactical vocabulary
for naming and misnaming violence.

The fact that political efforts of dissent and critique are
often labeled as "violent" by the very state authorities that
are threatened by those efforts is not a reason to despair of
language use. It means only that we have to expand and
refine the political vocabulary for thinking about violence
and the resistance to violence, taking account of how that
vocabulary is twisted and used to shield violent authorities against critique and opposition. When the critique of
continuing colonial violence is deemed violent (Palestine),

when a petition for peace is recast as an act of war (Turkey), when struggles for equality and freedom are construed as violent threats to state security (Black Lives Matter), or when "gender" is portrayed as a nuclear arsenal directed against the family (anti-gender ideology), then we are operating in the midst of politically consequential forms of phantasmagoria. To expose the ruse and strategy of those positions, we have to be in a position to track the ways that violence is reproduced at the level of a defensive rationale imbued with paranoia and hatred.

Nonviolence is less a failure of action than a physical assertion of the claims of life, a living assertion, a claim that is made by speech, gesture, and action, through networks, encampments, and assemblies; all of these seek to recast the living as worthy of value, as potentially grievable, precisely under conditions in which they are either erased from view or cast into irreversible forms of precarity. When the precarious expose their living status to those powers that threaten their very lives, they engage a form of persistence that holds the potential to defeat one of the guiding aims of violent power—namely, to cast those on the margins as dispensable, to push them beyond the margins into the zone of non-being, to use Fanon's phrase. When nonviolent movements work within the ideals of radical egalitarianism, it is the equal claim to a livable and grievable life that serves as a guiding social ideal, one that is fundamental to an ethics and politics of nonviolence that moves beyond the legacy of individualism. It opens up a new consideration of social freedom as defined in part by our constitutive interdependency. An egalitarian imaginary is required for such a struggle—one that reckons with the potential for destruction in every living bond. Violence against the other is, in this sense, violence against oneself, something that becomes clear when we recognize that violence assaults the living interdependency that is, or should be, our social world.

I

Nonviolence, Grievability, and the Critique of Individualism

Let us begin with the proposition that nonviolence becomes an ethical issue within the force field of violence itself. Nonviolence is perhaps best described as a practice of resistance that becomes possible, if not mandatory, precisely at the moment when doing violence seems most justified and obvious. In this way, it can be understood as a practice that not only stops a violent act, or a violent process, but requires a form of sustained action, sometimes aggressively pursued. So, one suggestion I will make is that we can think of nonviolence not simply as the absence of violence, or as the act of refraining from committing violence, but as a sustained commitment, even a way of rerouting aggression for the purposes of affirming ideals of equality and freedom. My first suggestion is that what Albert Einstein called "militant pacifism" might be rethought as aggressive nonviolence.[1] That

---

1   See Mary Whiton Calkins, "Militant Pacifism," *International Journal of Ethics* 28:1, 1917.

will involve rethinking the relation between aggression and violence, since the two are not the same. My second suggestion is that nonviolence does not make sense without a commitment to equality. The reason why nonviolence requires a commitment to equality can best be understood by considering that in this world some lives are more clearly valued than others, and that this inequality implies that certain lives will be more tenaciously defended than others. If one opposes the violence done to human lives—or, indeed, to other living beings—this presumes that it is because those lives are valuable. Our opposition affirms those lives as valuable. If they were to be lost as a result of violence, that loss would be *registered as a loss* only because those lives were affirmed as having a living value, and that, in turn, means we regard those lives as worthy of grief.

And yet, in this world, as we know, lives are not equally valued; their claim against being injured or killed is not always registered. And one reason for this is that their lives are not considered worthy of grief, or grievable. The reasons for this are many, and they include racism, xenophobia, homophobia and transphobia, misogyny, and the systemic disregard for the poor and the dispossessed. We live, in a daily way, with knowledge of nameless groups of people abandoned to death, on the borders of countries with closed borders, in the Mediterranean Sea, in countries where poverty and lack of access to food and health care has become overwhelming. If we seek to understand what nonviolence means now, in this world in which we live, we have to know the modalities of violence to be opposed, but we must also return to a fundamental set of questions that belong to our time: What makes a life valuable? What accounts for the unequal ways that lives are valued? And how might we begin to formulate an egalitarian imaginary that would become part of our practice of nonviolence—a practice of resistance, both vigilant and hopeful?

In this chapter, I turn to the problem of individualism in order to foreground the importance of social bonds and inter-dependency for understanding a non-individualist account of equality. And I will seek to link this idea of interdependency with nonviolence. In the following chapter, I will begin by asking about the resources of moral philosophy for develop-ing a reflective practice of nonviolence, and I will suggest that socially imbued fantasies enter into our moral reasoning on nonviolence such that we cannot always identify the demo-graphic assumptions we make about lives that are worth valuing, and those that are considered relatively or absolutely worthless. That second chapter moves from Immanuel Kant to Sigmund Freud and Melanie Klein. In the third chapter, I will consider the ethics and politics of nonviolence in light of contemporary forms of racism and social policy, suggesting that Frantz Fanon gives us a way to understand racial phan-tasms that informs the ethical dimension of biopolitics, and that Walter Benjamin's idea of an open-ended civil technique of conflict resolution (*Technik ziviler Übereinkunft*) gives us some way to think about living with and through conflict-ual relations without violent conclusions. To that end, I will suggest that aggression is a component part of social bonds based on interdependency, but that how aggression is crafted makes the difference for a practice that resists violence and that imagines a new future of social equality. The imagination—and what is imaginable—will turn out to be crucial for think-ing through this argument because we are at this moment ethically obliged and incited to think beyond what are treated as the realistic limits of the possible.

Some representatives of the history of liberal political thought would have us believe that we emerge into this
social and political world from a state of nature. And in that
state of nature, we are already, for some reason, individuals,
and we are in conflict with one another. We are not given to
understand how we became individuated, nor are we told
precisely why conflict is the first of our passionate relations,
rather than dependency or attachment. The Hobbesian view,
which has been the most influential in shaping our understanding of political contracts, tells us that one individual
wants what another has, or that both individuals lay claim
to the same territory, and that they fight with one another to
pursue their selfish aims and to establish their personal right
to property, to nature, and to social dominance. Of course,
the state of nature was always a fiction, as Jean-Jacques
Rousseau openly conceded, but it has been a powerful fiction,
a mode of imagining that becomes possible under conditions of what Karl Marx called "political economy." It functions in many ways: for instance, it gives us a counterfactual
condition by which to assess our contemporary situation;
and it offers a point of view, in the way that science fiction
does, from which to see the specificity and contingency of
the political organization of space and time, of passions and
interests, in the present. Writing on Rousseau, literary critic
Jean Starobinski opined that the state of nature provides an
imaginary framework in which there is only one individual
in the scene: self-sufficient, without dependency, saturated
in self-love yet without any need for another.[2] Indeed, where

_____

2   Jean Starobinski, *Jean-Jacques Rousseau: Transparency and Obstruction*,
Chicago: University of Chicago Press, 1988.

there are no other persons to speak of, there is no problem of equality; but once other living human creatures enter the scene, the problem of equality and conflict immediately emerges. Why is that the case?

Marx criticized that part of the state of nature hypothesis that posits the individual as primary. In his *Economic and Philosophic Manuscripts of 1844*, he ridiculed, with great irony, the notion that in the beginning humans are, like Robinson Crusoe, alone on an island, providing for their own sustenance, living without dependency on others, without systems of labor, and without any common organization of political and economic life. Marx writes: "Let us not put ourselves in that fictitious primordial state like a political economist trying to clarify things. It merely pushes the issue into a gray, misty distance . . . We proceed from a present fact of political economy."[3] Marx thought he could discard fiction in favor of present fact, but that did not stop him from making use of those very fictions to develop his critique of political economy. They do not represent reality, but if we know how to read such fictions, they yield a commentary on present reality that we otherwise might not achieve. One enters the fiction in order to discern the structure, but also to ask: What can and cannot be figured here? What can be imagined, and through what terms?

For instance, that lonely and self-sufficient figure of Robinson Crusoe was invariably an adult and a man, the first figure of the "natural man"—the one whose

---

3 Karl Marx, *Writings of the Young Marx on Philosophy and Society*, eds. Lloyd Easton and Kurt Guddat, Garden City, NY: Anchor Books, 1967, 288–9.

self-sufficiency is eventually interrupted by the demands
of social and economic life, but not as a consequence of
his natural condition. Indeed, when others enter the scene,
conflict begins—or so the story goes. So, in the beginning
(temporally considered) and most fundamentally (ontologi-
cally considered), individuals pursue their selfish interests,
they clash and fight, but conflict becomes arbitrated only
in the midst of a regulated sociality, since each individual
would presumably, prior to entering the social contract, seek
to pursue and satisfy his wants, regardless of their effect on
others and without any expectation of resolution, without
resolving those competing or clashing desires. The contract
thus emerges, according to this fiction, first and foremost as
a means of conflict resolution. Each individual must restrict
his desires, put limits on his capacity to consume, to take,
and to act, in order to live according to commonly binding laws. For Hobbes, those laws become the "common
power" by which human nature is restrained. The state of
nature was not exactly an ideal, and Hobbes did not call for
a "return" to that state (as Rousseau sometimes did), for he
imagined that lives would be cut short, that murder would
be unrestrained if there were no common government and
no binding set of laws to subdue the conflictual character
of human nature. The state of nature was for him a war,
but not a war among states or existing authorities. Rather,
it was a war waged by one sovereign individual against
another— a war, we might add, of individuals who regarded
themselves as sovereign. For it is unclear whether that sovereignty belonged to an individual conceived of as separate
from the state, who transferred his own sovereignty to the
state, or if the state was already operating as the implicit

horizon of this imaginary. The political-theological concept of sovereignty precedes and conditions the attribution or suspension of sovereign status to the individual, that is, it produces, through that conferral, the figure of the sovereign subject.

Let us be clear: the state of nature differs among Locke, Rousseau, and Hobbes, and even within Hobbes's *Leviathan*, there are arguably at least five versions.[4] The state of nature can postulate a time before society; it can seek to describe foreign civilizations that are assumed to be premodern; it can offer a political psychology that accounts for civil strife; it can describe political power dynamics within seventeenth-century Europe. I am not exactly conducting a scholarly review, but I do want to consider how the state of nature becomes the occasion for a certain kind of imagining, if not a fantasy or what Rousseau calls "a pure fiction," then one that is centrally concerned with violent conflict and its resolution.[5] As such, we can ask: Under what historical conditions

---

4 According to Gregory Sadler, there is "a rhetorical construct 'state of nature' as war of all against all, lacking any institutions of civilization and civil society; Historically existent 'state(s) of nature' in pre-political societies, where family, patron-client, clan, or tribal structures are in conflict with each other; Historically existent 'state(s) of nature' within established civil societies where, despite establishment and enforcement of laws, citizens remain in a mistrustful condition vis-à-vis each other, i.e. concerned about criminality; The historically existent 'state of nature' governing foreign relations, i.e. the condition of states in relation to each other; Historically existent and possible 'state(s)' of nature that culminate in civil war with the breakdown of civil society through factionalization." Gregory Sadler, "Five States of Nature in Hobbes's Leviathan," *Oxford Philosopher*, March 2016.

5 Jean-Jacques Rousseau, *The Political Writings of Jean-Jacques Rousseau*, ed. C. E. Vaughan, Cambridge, UK: Cambridge University Press, 1915, 286.

do such fictions or fantasies take hold? They become possible and persuasive from within a condition of social conflict or as a consequence of its history; they represent, perhaps, the dream of an escape from the sufferings associated with the capitalist organization of work, or they function as a justification for that very organization. These imaginings articulate, and comment upon, the arguments for strengthening state power and its instruments of violence to cultivate or contain the popular will; they emerge in our understanding of populism, the condition in which the popular will is imagined to assume an unconstrained form or to rebel against established structures; they encode and reproduce forms of domination and exploitation that set classes and religious or racial groups against one another, as if "tribalism" were a primitive or natural condition that rears up and explodes if states fail to exercise restraining powers—that is, if states fail to impose their own violence, including legal violence.

In the course of this text, we will distinguish between fantasy, understood as a conscious wish that can be individual or shared, and phantasy, which has an unconscious dimension and often operates according to a syntax that requires interpretation. The daydream can hover on the border between the conscious and unconscious, but Phantasy, as developed first by Susan Isaacs (1948) and elaborated by Melanie Klein, tends to include a complex unconscious set of relations to objects. Unconscious fantasy became one basis for the Lacanian notion of the imaginary, designating unconscious tendencies that take form as images and that pull us apart or in different directions, and against which narcissistic defenses are erected. In Laplanche, fantasy is defined somewhat differently and in two distinct ways: first, as an "imaginary scene in which the subject is a protagonist, representing the fulfillment of a wish (in the last analysis, an unconscious wish) in a manner that is distorted to a greater or lesser extent by defensive processes";[6] secondly, in his discussion of "*Fantasme*" he makes clear that we are not confronting a distinction between imagination and reality, but a structuring psychic modality by which reality itself is invariably interpreted. Thus, he proposes a reformulation of psychoanalytic doctrine with the idea of "original fantasy" (what Freud called "*Urphantasien*"), which structures modes of perceiving, and operates according to its own syntactical rules. Thus, the original phantasy takes form as a scene with multiple actors disposed by vectors of desire and aggression. This last notion allows us to consider what is happening in "the state of nature" considered not only as a fiction or a conscious fantasy, but as a phantasmatic scene structured by multiple occluded determinants. In the following, I seek to reserve "fantasy" for most of the scenes of violence and defense that I consider, but in relation to Klein, where the term "phantasy" maintains a distinctly unconscious dimension, I reserve that spelling. I use the terms "phantasmatic" and "phantasmagoric" to consider the interplay of socially shared, or communicable, unconscious and conscious fantasies that take the form of a scene but do not for that reason presuppose a collective unconscious.

If we understand the state of nature as a fiction or, rather, a phantasy (and the two are not the same, as we shall see),

---

6 Jean Laplanche and J.-B. Pontalis, *The Language of Psycho-Analysis*, New York: W. W. Norton, 1967, 314.

then what set of wishes or desires does it represent or articulate? I suggest that these wishes belong neither simply to the individual nor to an autonomous psychic life, but maintain a critical relation to the social and economic condition upon which they comment. This relation can function as an inverted picture, a critical commentary, a justification, or, indeed, a ruthless critique. What is posited as an origin or an original condition is retrospectively imagined, and so posited as the result of a sequence that begins in the already-constituted social world. And yet, there is a yearning to posit a foundation, an imaginary origin, as a way to account for this world, or perhaps to escape its pain and alienation. This train of thought could easily lead us down a psychoanalytic path if we were to take seriously the idea that *unconscious forms of phantasy* function as a *foundation* for human psychic life in relation to its social world. This may well be true. However, my desire is not to replace fantasy with reality, but to learn how to read such a fantasy as yielding key insights into the structure and dynamic of historically constituted organizations of power and violence as they relate to life and to death. Indeed, I myself will not be able to offer a critical rejoinder to this notion of a "man without needs" at the origin of social life without engaging a conjecture of my own: one that does not start with me, but takes me up into its terms, articulating, as it were, the syntax of the social through a different imaginary.

One rather remarkable feature of this state of nature fantasy, which is regularly invoked as a "foundation," is that, in the beginning, apparently, there is a man and he is an adult and he is on his own, self-sufficient. So let's take notice that this story begins not at the origin, but in the middle of a history that is *not* about to be told: with the opening moment of the story, that is, with the moment that marks the beginning, gender, for instance, has already been decided. Independence and dependency have been separated, and masculine and feminine are determined, in part, in relation to this distribution of dependency. The primary and founding figure of the human is masculine. That comes as no surprise; masculinity is defined by its lack of dependency (and that is not exactly news, but it continues somehow to be quite startling). But what does seem interesting, and it is as true for Hobbes as it is for Marx, is that the human is from the start an adult.

In other words, the individual who is introduced to us as the first moment of the human, the outbreak of the human onto the world, is posited as if he was never a child; as if he was never provided for, never depended upon parents or kinship relations, or upon social institutions, in order to survive and grow and (presumably) learn. That individual has already been cast as a gender, but not by a social assignment; rather, it is because he is an *individual*—and the social form of the individual is masculine in this scene—that he is a man. So, if we wish to understand this fantasy, we have to ask what version of the human and what version of gender it represents, and what occlusions are required for that representation to work. Dependency is, as it were, written out of the picture of the original man; he is somehow, and from the start, always and already upright, capable, without ever having been supported by others, without having held onto another's body in order to steady himself, without ever having been fed when he could not feed himself, without ever having been wrapped in a blanket for warmth by someone else.[7] He sprang, lucky guy, from the imaginations of liberal theorists as a full adult, without relations, but equipped with anger and desire, sometimes capable of a happiness or self-sufficiency that depended on a natural world preemptively void of other people. Shall we then concede that an annihilation has taken place prior to the narrated scene, that an annihilation inaugurates the scene: everyone else is excluded, negated, and from the start? Is this perhaps an inaugural violence? It is not a tabula rasa, but a slate *wiped clean*. But so too is the prehistory of the so-called state of nature. Since the state of nature is supposed to be, in one of its most influential variants, a prehistory of social and economic life, the annihilation of alterity constitutes the prehistory of this prehistory, suggesting that we are not only elaborating a fantasy, but giving a history of that very fantasy—arguably, a murder that leaves no trace.

The social contract, as many feminist theorists have argued, is already *a sexual contract*.[8] But, even before women enter the picture, there is only this individual man. There is somewhere a woman in the scene, but she does not take form as a figure. We cannot even fault the representation of women in the scene, because she is unrepresentable. An expulsion of some sort has taken place, and within that vacated place is erected the adult man. He is assumed to desire women in the course of things, but even this postulated heterosexuality is free of dependency and rests on a

---

7   See Adriana Cavarero, *Inclinations: A Critique of Rectitude*, Stanford, CA: Stanford University Press, 2016.

8   Carole Pateman, *The Sexual Contract*, Stanford, CA: Stanford University Press, 1988. See also various responses to Pateman: "The Sexual Contract Thirty Years On," *Feminist Legal Studies* 26:1, 2018, 93–104.

cultivated amnesia regarding its formation. He is understood to encounter others first in a conflictual way.

Why bother with this influential phantasmatic scene in political theory? After all, my topic is the ethics and politics of nonviolence. I am not actually going to argue against the primary character of conflictual relations. In fact, I will insist that conflict is a potential part of every social bond, and that Hobbes is not altogether wrong. Indeed, Freud harbors a Hobbesian thesis when he challenges the biblical commandment to honor thy neighbor and not covet his wife; for why, Freud asks, should we not assume that enmity and hostility are more fundamental than love? My thesis, which will arrive a bit later, is that if nonviolence is to make sense as an ethical and political position, it cannot simply repress aggression or do away with its reality; rather, nonviolence emerges as a meaningful concept precisely when destruction is most likely or seems most certain. When destruction becomes the ardent aim of desire but is nevertheless checked, what accounts for that check, that imposition of a limit and displacement? From where does it come, and what lets it take hold and be maintained? Some would say that the check is always a form of self-checking—that it is the super-ego that checks the externalization of aggression, even as "the super-ego" is the name we have for the process of absorbing aggression into the architecture of the psyche. The economy of the super-ego is a moralism whereby aggression unleashes itself against itself in an intensifying double bind that weighs down upon the psychic life that bears this recursive structure of self-negation. It denounces violence, and that denunciation becomes a new form of violence in the course of things. Others would say that this check on violence can only be applied from the outside, by law, by government, even the police; that is the more properly Hobbesian view. In this view, the coercive power of the state is necessary to contain the potentially murderous rage of its unruly subjects. Others claim that there is a calm or pacific region of the soul, and that we must cultivate the capacity to dwell always there, subduing aggression and destructiveness through religious or ethical practices or rituals. But, as I noted, Einstein argued in favor of a "militant pacifism," and perhaps now we can ourselves talk about an aggressive form of nonviolence. To understand this, I propose that we think first about an ethics of nonviolence that presupposes forms of dependency, and interdependency, that are unmanageable or that become the source of conflict and aggression. Second, I propose that we consider how our understanding of equality relates to the ethics and politics of nonviolence. For that connection to make sense, we would have to admit into our idea of political equality the equal grievability of lives. For only a departure from a presumptive individualism will let us understand the possibility of an aggressive nonviolence: one that emerges in the midst of conflict, one that takes hold in the force field of violence itself. That means such an equality is not simply the equality of individuals with one another, but a concept that first becomes thinkable once a critique of individualism is waged.

Dependency and Obligation

Let us, then, try a different story. It begins this way: every individual emerges in the course of the process of individuation. No one is born an individual; if someone becomes an individual over time, he or she does not escape the fundamental conditions of dependency in the course of that process. That condition cannot be escaped by way of time. We were all, regardless of our political viewpoints in the present, born into a condition of radical dependency. As we reflect back on that condition as adults, perhaps we are slightly insulted or alarmed, or perhaps we dismiss the thought. Perhaps someone with a strong sense of individual self-sufficiency will indeed be offended by the fact that there was a time when one could not feed oneself or could not stand on one's own. I want to suggest, however, that no one actually stands on one's own; strictly speaking, no one feeds oneself. Disability studies has shown us that in order to move along the street, there must be pavement that allows for movement, especially if one only moves with a chair or with an instrument for support.[9] But the pavement is also an instrument for support, as are the traffic lights and the curb stops. It is not only those who are disabled who require support in order to move, to be fed, or indeed, to breathe. All of these basic human capacities are supported in one way or another. No one moves or breathes or finds food who is not supported by a world that provides an environment built for passage, that prepares and distributes food so that it makes its way to our mouths, a world that sustains the environment that makes possible air of a quality that we can breathe.

Dependency can be defined partly as a reliance on social and material structures and on the environment, for the latter, too, makes life possible. But regardless of our quarrels

---

9   See Jos Boys, ed., *Disability, Space, Architecture: A Reader*, New York: Routledge, 2017.

with psychoanalysis—and what is psychoanalysis but a theory and practice with which people quarrel—perhaps we can say that we do not overcome the dependency of infancy when we become adults. That does not mean that the adult is dependent in the exact same way that the infant is, but only that we have become creatures who constantly imagine a self-sufficiency, only to find that image of ourselves undermined repeatedly in the course of life. This is, of course, a Lacanian position, articulated most famously by the "mirror stage"—the jubilant boy who thinks he stands on his own as he looks in the mirror, and yet, watching him, we know that the mother, or some obscured object-support (*trotte-bébé*), holds him in front of the mirror as he rejoices in his radical self-sufficiency.[10] Perhaps we can say that the founding conceits of liberal individualism are a kind of mirror stage, that they take place within an imaginary of this kind. What support, what dependency, has to be disavowed for the fantasy of self-sufficiency to take hold, for the story to start with a timeless adult masculinity?

The implication of this scene, of course, is that it would seem that masculinity is identified with a phantasmatic self-sufficiency, while femininity is identified with the support she provides, a support regularly disavowed. This picture and story lock us into an economy of gender relations that hardly serves us. Heterosexuality becomes the presumptive frame, and it is derived from the theory of mother and child, which is but one way of imagining the relations of support for the child. The gendered structure of the family is taken

---

10 Jacques Lacan, "The Mirror Stage as Formative of the 'I' Function," in *Écrits*, trans. Bruce Fink, New York and London: Norton, 2006, 75–81.

for granted, including, of course, the obscuring of the mother's labor of care and the full absence of the father. And if we accept all this as the symbolic structure of things rather than merely a specific imaginary, we accept the operation of a law that can only be changed in incremental fashion and over a very long time. The theory that describes this fantasy, this asymmetry, and this gendered division of labor can end up reproducing and validating its terms, unless it shows us another way out, unless it asks about the scene prior to, or outside of, the scene—the moment, as it were, before the beginning.

Let us now move from dependency to interdependency, and ask how that alters our understanding of vulnerability, of conflict, adulthood, sociality, violence, and politics. I ask this question because, at both a political and an economic level, the facts of global interdependency are denied. Or they are exploited. Of course, advertisements for corporations celebrate a globalized world, but that idea of corporate expansion captures only one sense of globalization. National sovereignty may be waning, and yet new nationalisms insist upon the frame.[11] So one reason it is so difficult to convince governments such as that of the United States that global warming is a real threat to the future of the livable world is that their rights to expand production and markets, to exploit nature, to profit, remain centered on the augmentation of a national wealth and power. Perhaps they do not conceive of the possibility that what they do affects all regions of the world, and that what happens in all regions

---

11 Wendy Brown, *Walled States: Waning Sovereignty*, New York: Zone Books, 2010.

of the world affects the very possibility of the continuation of a livable environment, one on which we all depend. Or perhaps they do know that they are in the midst of a globally destructive activity, and that too seems to them like a right, a power, a prerogative that should be compromised by nothing and no one.

The idea of global obligations that serve all inhabitants of the world, human and animal, is about as far from the neoliberal consecration of individualism as it could be, and yet it is regularly dismissed as naive. So I am summoning my courage to expose my naiveté, my fantasy—my counter-fantasy, if you will. Some people ask, in more or less incredulous tones: "How can you believe in global obligations? That is surely naive." But, when I ask if they want to live in a world where no one argues for global obligations, they usually say no. I argue that only by avowing this interdependency does it become possible to formulate global obligations, including obligations toward migrants; toward the Roma; those who live in precarious situations, or indeed, those who are subject to occupation and war; those who are subject to institutional and systemic racism; the indigenous whose murder and disappearance never surface fully in the public record; women who are subject to domestic and public violence, and harassment in the workplace; and gender nonconforming people who are exposed to bodily harm, including incarceration and death. I want to suggest, as well, that a new idea of equality can only emerge from a more fully imagined interdependency, an imagining that unfolds in practices and institutions, in new forms of civic and political life. Oddly enough, equality imagined in this way compels us to rethink what we mean by an equality *among* individuals. Of course, it is good that one person is treated as equal to another. (I am all in favor of anti-discrimination law; don't get me wrong.) But that formulation, as important as it is, does not tell us by virtue of what set of relationships social and political equality becomes thinkable. It takes the individual person as the unit of analysis and then establishes a comparison. When equality is understood as an individual right (as it is in the right to equal treatment), it is separated from the social obligations we bear toward one another. To formulate equality on the basis of the relations that define our enduring social existence, that define us as social living creatures, is to make a social claim—a collective claim on society, if not a claim to the social as the framework within which our imaginings of equality, freedom, and justice take form and make sense. Whatever claims of equality are then formulated, they emerge from the relations *between* people, in the name of those relations and those bonds, but not as features of an individual subject.[12] Equality is thus a feature of social relations that depends for its articulation on an increasingly *avowed* interdependency—letting go of the body as a "unit" in order to understand one's boundaries as relational and social predicaments: including sources of joy, susceptibility to violence, sensitivity to heat and cold, tentacular yearnings for food, sociality, and sexuality.

I have argued elsewhere that "vulnerability" should not be considered as a subjective state, but rather as a feature of our shared or interdependent lives.[13] We are never simply

12 For a strong analytic view on relational equality, see Elizabeth Anderson, "What Is the Point of Equality?," *Ethics* 109:2, 1999, 287–337.

13 See my "Rethinking Vulnerability and Resistance," in Judith Butler,

vulnerable, but always vulnerable to a situation, a person, a social structure, something upon which we rely and in relation to which we are exposed. Perhaps we can say that we are vulnerable to those environmental and social structures that make our lives possible, and that when they falter, so do we. To be dependent implies vulnerability: one is vulnerable to the social structure upon which one depends, so if the structure fails, one is exposed to a precarious condition. If that is so, we are not talking about my vulnerability or yours, but rather a feature of the relation that binds us to one another and to the larger structures and institutions upon which we depend for the continuation of life. Vulnerability is not exactly the same as dependency. I depend on someone, something, or some condition in order to live. But when that person disappears, or that object is withdrawn, or that social institution falls apart, I am vulnerable to being dispossessed, abandoned, or exposed in ways that may well prove unlivable. The relational understanding of vulnerability shows that we are not altogether separable from the conditions that make our lives possible or impossible. In other words, because we cannot exist liberated from such conditions, we are never fully individuated.

One implication of this view is that the obligations that bind us to one another follow from the condition of interdependency that makes our lives possible but that can also be one condition for exploitation and violence. The political organization of life itself requires that interdependency—and the equality it implies—is acknowledged through policy,

Zeynep Gambetti, and Leticia Sabsay, eds., *Vulnerability in Resistance*, Durham, NC: Duke University Press, 2016.

institution, civil society, and government. If we accept the proposal that there are, or must be, global obligations—that is to say, obligations that are globally shared and ought to be considered binding—they cannot be reduced to obligations that nation-states have toward one another. They would have to be post-national in character, traversing borders and navigating their terms, since populations at the border or crossing the border (stateless people, refugees) are included in the larger network of interrelationships implied by global obligations.

I have been arguing that the task, as I imagine it, is not to overcome dependency in order to achieve self-sufficiency, but to accept interdependency as a condition of equality. That formulation meets with an immediate and important challenge. After all, there are forms of colonial power that seek to establish the so-called "dependency" of the colonized, and these kinds of arguments seek to make dependency an essential, pathological feature of populations who have been colonized.[14] That deployment of dependency confirms both racism and colonialism; it identifies the cause of a group's subordination as a psycho-social feature of the group itself. The colonizer, then, as French-Tunisian novelist and essayist Albert Memmi has argued, understands himself as the adult in the scene, the one who can bring a colonized population out of their "childlike" dependency into an enlightened adulthood.[15] We find this figure of the colonized as

---

14 Nancy Fraser and Linda Gordon, "A Genealogy of Dependency: Tracing a Keyword of the US Welfare State," *Signs* 19:2, 1994, 309–36.

15 Albert Memmi, *La dépendance: Esquisse pour un portrait du dépendant*, Paris: Gallimard, 1979; translated by Phillip A. Facey as *Dependence: A Sketch for a Portrait of the Dependent*, Boston: Beacon Press, 1984.

the child requiring tutelage in Kant's famous essay "What Is Enlightenment?" But the truth is that the colonizer depends upon the colonized, for when the colonized refuse to remain subordinate, then the colonizer is threatened with the loss of colonial power. On the one hand, it looks good to over-come dependency if one has been made dependent on a colonial structure, or made dependent on an unjust state, or an exploitative marriage. Breaking with those forms of subjection are part of the process of emancipation, of claim-ing both equality and freedom. But which version of equal-ity do we then accept? And which version of freedom? If we break the ties of dependency in an effort to overcome subjec-tion and exploitation, does that mean that we now value independence? Well, yes, it does. Yet, if that independence is modeled on mastery and so becomes a way of breaking ties with those forms of interdependency that we value, what then follows? If independence returns us to the sovereignty of the individual or of the state in such a way that post-sover-eign understandings of cohabitation become unthinkable, then we have returned to a version of self-sufficiency that implies endless conflict. After all, it is only from a renewed and revalued notion of interdependency among regions and hemispheres that we can begin to think about the threat to the environment, the problem of the global slum, systemic racism, the condition of stateless people whose migration is a common global responsibility, even the more thorough overcoming of colonial modes of power. And that we can begin to formulate another view of social solidarity and of nonviolence.

Throughout this book, I move between a psychoanalytic and a social understanding of interdependency, laying the groundwork for a practice of nonviolence within a new egal-itarian imaginary. These levels of analysis have to be brought together without assuming the psychoanalytic framework as a model for all social relations. The critique of ego psychol-ogy, however, does give a social meaning to psychoanalysis that links it with a broader consideration of the conditions of sustenance and persistence—questions central to any conception of the biopolitical. My counter-thesis to the state of nature hypothesis is that no body can sustain itself on its own. The body is not, and never was, a self-subsisting kind of being, which is but one reason why the metaphysics of substance—which conceives the body as an extended being with discrete boundaries—was never a particularly good frame for understanding what a body is; the body is given over to others in order to persist; it is given over to some other set of hands before it can make use of its own. Does metaphysics have a way to conceptualize this vital paradox? As interpersonal as this relation may sound, it is also socially organized in a broader sense, pointing as it does to the social organization of life. We all start by being given over—a situ-ation both passive and animating. That's what happens when a child is born: someone gives the child over to someone else. We are, from the start, handled against our will in part because the will is in the process of being formed. Even the infant Oedipus was handed over to that shepherd who was supposed to let him die of exposure on the side of the hill. That was a nearly fatal act, since his mother handed him to someone tasked with arranging to let him die. Being handed over against one's will is not always a beautiful scene. The infant is given over by someone to someone else, and the caregiver is conventionally understood as given over to the task of care—given over in a way that may not be experienced as an act of deliberate will or choice. Care is not always consensual, and it does not always take the form of a contract: it can be a way of getting wrecked, time and again, by the demands of a wailing and hungry creature. But there is here a larger claim that does not rely on any particular account of the social organization of motherhood or caregiving. Our enduring dependency on social and economic forms of support for life itself is not something we grow out of—it is not a dependency that converts to independence in time. When there is nothing to depend upon, when social structures fail or are withdrawn, then life itself falters or fails: life becomes precarious. That enduring condition may become more poignant in care for children and the elderly, or for those who are physically challenged, but all of us are subject to this condition.

What does it mean "to be given over"? And does it imply that we are also those to whom someone is given over? Are we at once given over, and those to whom others are given over—a kind of asymmetry for each that is nevertheless a reciprocity when regarded as a social relation? When the world fails us, when we ourselves become worldless in the social sense, the body suffers and shows its precarity; that mode of demonstrating precarity is itself, or carries with it, a political demand and even an expression of outrage. To be a body differentially exposed to harm or to death is precisely to exhibit a form of precarity, but also to suffer a form of inequality that is unjust. So, the situation of many populations who are increasingly subject to unlivable precarity raises for us the question of global obligations. If we ask why any of us should care about those who suffer at a distance

from us, the answer is not to be found in paternalistic justifications, but in the fact that we inhabit the world together in
relations of interdependency. Our fates are, as it were, given
over to one another.

So, we have moved far from the Robinson Crusoe
figure with which we began. For the embodied subject is
defined, on the contrary, by its lack of self-sufficiency. And
this also gives us some indication of how longing, desire,
rage, and anxiety all figure in this scene, especially under
conditions when exposure becomes unbearable, or dependency becomes unmanageable. Suffering those conditions can
lead to understandable rage. Under what conditions does
interdependency become a scene of aggression, conflict, and
violence? How do we understand the destructive potential of
this social bond?

Violence and Nonviolence

Moral philosophers and theologians have asked: What
grounds the claims that killing is wrong, and that the interdiction against killing is justified? The usual way of handling
this question is to ask whether that interdiction, commandment, or prohibition is absolute; whether it has a theological
or other conventional status; whether it is a matter of law
or one of morality. It is also invariably accompanied by a
further question, namely, whether there are bona fide exceptions to such an interdiction, when injuring or even killing is
justified. And then debates tend to ensue about what, if any,
exceptions exist, and what they indicate about the less-than-
absolute character of that interdiction. Self-defense usually
enters the debate at this juncture.

The exception to the rule is important, perhaps more so than the rule itself. For instance, if there are exceptions to the prohibition on killing, and if there are *always* such exceptions, this suggests that the prohibition against killing is less than absolute. It is a prohibition that on occasion fails to assert itself, or holds itself back, or suspends its own powers of restraint.

"Self-defense" is a highly ambiguous term, as we can see in militaristic modes of foreign policy that justify every attack as self-defense, and in contemporary US law that now makes provisions for preemptive killing. It can, and in practice does, extend to the defense of loved ones, children or animals, or others who are considered close to you—relations that are part of one's broader sense of self. It therefore makes sense to ask what defines and limits those relations, what elaborates the conception of self to include groups of others in this way, and why they are usually understood as biological relatives or those related through conjugal ties. A rather arbitrary and dubious distinction emerges between those who are close to oneself—in the name of whose protection one may commit violence, even murder—and those who are at a distance from oneself—in the name of whom, in whose defense, one *may not* kill. So, what and who is part of the self that you are, and what relations are included under the rubric of the "self" to be defended? Are we more ethically obligated to preserve the lives of those who are close to us than to stand for the lives of those who are considered far away, whether in a geographical, economic, or cultural sense?

If I defend myself and those who are considered part of myself (or proximate enough so that I know and love them), then this self that I am is relational, yes; but such relations, considered as belonging to the region of the self, are limited to those who are proximate and similar. One is justified in using violence to defend those who belong to the region or regime of the self. Some group is, then, covered by my expanded claims of self-defense, and they are understood to be worthy of a violent protection against violence: that is, a violence done to others so that it is not done to one's own. The interdiction against violence reemerges within the exception. The interdiction now is imposed on the other group, the one that is *not* part of my region of the self, not to engage in violent acts. And absent that operative interdiction, I, or we, are apparently justified in killing.

Further, when we get to that point when one, or one's group, violently defends what it takes to be its "self" against violence, not only is a rather large and consequential exception made to the interdiction against violence, but the distinction starts to collapse between the force of the interdiction and the violence interdicted. The exception to the interdiction opens up onto a situation of *war*, in which it is always right to defend oneself or one's own violently and in the name of self-defense, but certainly not to defend a whole host of others who do not belong to one's self. And this means that there will always be those whose lives I do *not* defend, and there will always be those who seek to do violence to those whose lives are intricately bound up with my own, part of my extended region of the self, which would include those others I recognize as having a binding ethical claim upon me. At such moments, the interdiction against violence again proves itself to be less than absolute. And the exception to the interdiction becomes a potential state of war, or at least such a state is coextensive with its logic. If one will kill for this or that person who is proximate and affiliated, what finally distinguishes the proximate from the non-proximate, and under what conditions could that distinction be regarded as ethically justifiable?

Of course, international human rights interventionists, including those we call "liberal hawks" in the United States, would argue that it follows that we, especially in the First World, should always be prepared to go to war for everyone. But my point is decidedly different. The exceptions to the norm of nonviolence actually begin to elaborate forms of group identification, even nationalism, that result in a certain war logic. It goes like this: I am willing to defend those who are *like* me, or who might be understood as part of the generalized regime of myself, but not to defend those who are unlike me, which converts rather easily into the claim: I will defend only those who are like me, or recognizable to me, but will defend *against* those who are not recognizable to me and with whom no ties of belonging seem to exist. With these examples, one question I am trying to pose is whether there is a norm that is invoked to distinguish those who belong to the group whose lives are worth saving from those who do not belong to that group and whose lives are not worth saving or defending. For implicit in the way the exception to the interdiction against violence works is that there are those who are understood to belong and to deserve protection against violence, whereas in relation to those who do not belong, one may well invoke one's principle of nonviolence and decline to intervene on their behalf.

Although that may sound cynical, the point is meant only to foreground the fact that some of our moral principles may well be already in the sway of other political interests and frameworks. The distinction between populations that are worth violently defending and those that are not implies that some lives are simply considered more valuable than others. So, my suggestion has been to consider that the principle by which the exception to nonviolence is identified is at once also a measure for distinguishing among populations: those one is *not* ready to grieve, or that do not qualify as grievable; and those one *is* prepared to grieve, and whose death ought in all instances to be forestalled.

So, if we make exceptions to the principle of nonviolence, it shows that we are ready to fight and to harm, possibly even to murder, and that we are prepared to give moral reasons for doing so. According to this logic, one does this either in self-defense, or in defense of those who belong to a wider regime of the self—those with whom identification is possible or who are recognized to constitute the broader social or political domain of selves to which one's own self belongs. And, if that last proposition is true (that there are those I am willing to hurt or murder, in the name of those with whom I share a social identity or whom I love in some way that is essential to who I am), then there is a moral justification for violence that emerges precisely on a demographic basis.

What is demography doing in the midst of this moral debate about exceptions to the interdiction against violence? I am suggesting simply that what starts as a moral framework for understanding nonviolence turns into a different kind of problem—a political problem. In the first instance, the norm we invoke to distinguish lives we are willing to defend from those that are effectively dispensable is part of a larger operation of biopower that unjustifiably distinguishes between grievable and ungrievable lives.

But if we accept the notion that all lives are equally grievable, and thus that the political world ought rightly to be organized in such a way that this principle is affirmed by economic and institutional life, then we arrive at a different conclusion and perhaps at another way to approach the problem of nonviolence. After all, if a life, from the start, is regarded as grievable, then every precaution will be taken to preserve and to safeguard that life against harm and destruction. In other words, what we might call the "radical equality of the grievable" could be understood as the demographic precondition for an ethics of nonviolence that does not make the exception. I am not saying that no one should defend oneself, or that there are no cases where intervention is necessary. For nonviolence is not an absolute principle, but an open-ended struggle with violence and its countervailing forces.

I would like to suggest that a thoroughly *egalitarian approach to the preservation of life* imports a perspective of radical democracy into the ethical consideration of how best to practice nonviolence. Within such an imaginary, such an experiment that looks at the world in this way, there would be no difference between lives worth preserving and lives that are potentially grievable. Grievability governs the way in which living creatures are managed, and it proves to be an integral dimension of biopolitics and of ways of thinking about equality among the living. My further claim is that this argument in favor of equality bears directly on the ethics and politics of nonviolence. A nonviolent practice may well include a prohibition against killing, but it is not reducible to that prohibition. For instance, one response to a "pro-life" position is to argue first for the equal value of life, and to show that the "pro-life" position is actually committed to gender *inequality*, attributing an embryonic life with the right to life while decimating the legitimate claims that women make to their own lives in the name of freedom and equality. Such a "pro-life" position is incompatible with social equality, and intensifies the differential between the grievable and the ungrievable. Once again, women become the ungrievable.

If our ethical and political practices remain restricted to an individual mode of life or decision making, or to a virtue ethics that reflects on who we are as individuals, we risk losing sight of that social and economic interdependency that establishes an embodied version of equality. In turn, this condition exposes us to the possibility of abandonment or destructiveness, but it also delineates the ethical obligations to thwart those consequences.

What difference to our thinking would such a framework imply? Most forms of violence are committed to inequality, whether or not that commitment is explicitly thematized. And the framing of the decision whether or not to use violence, on any given occasion, makes a number of assumptions about those with regard to whom violence is to be waged or not. For instance, it is impossible to comply with an interdiction against violence if one cannot name or know the living creature that is not to be killed. If the person, the group, the population is not considered already living and alive, how is the command not to kill to be understood? It makes sense to assume that only those who are considered living can be effectively named and safeguarded by an interdiction against violence. But a second point is also necessary.

If the interdiction against killing rests on the presumption that all lives are valuable—that they bear value *as lives*, in their status as living beings—then the universality of the claim only holds on the condition that value extends equally to all living beings. This means that we have to think not only about persons, but animals; and not only about living creatures, but living processes, the systems and forms of life.

There is a third point: a life has to be grievable—that is, its loss has to be conceptualizable *as a loss*—for an interdiction against violence and destruction to include that life among those living beings to be safeguarded from violence. The condition under which some lives are more grievable than others means that the condition of equality cannot be met. The consequence is that a prohibition against killing, for instance, applies only to those lives that are grievable, but not to those who are considered ungrievable (those who are considered already lost, and thus never fully alive). In this way, the differential distribution of grievability has to be addressed if an ethics of nonviolence is to presume and affirm the equal value of lives. Thus, the unequal distribution of grievability might be one framework for understanding the differential production of humans and other creatures within a structure of inequality, or, indeed, within a structure of violent disavowal. To claim that equality formally extends to all humans is to sidestep the fundamental question of how the human is produced, or, rather, who is produced as a recognizable and valuable human, and who is not. For equality to make sense as a concept, it must imply such formal extension to all humans, but even then, we make an assumption about who is included within the category of the human, and who is partially included, or fully excluded;

who is fully alive or partially dead; who would be grieved if they were lost, and who would not be grieved, because they are, effectively, socially dead. For that reason, we cannot take the human as the ground of our analysis, nor can we take as its foundation the state of nature: the human is a historically variable concept, differentially articulated in the context of inegalitarian forms of social and political power; the field of the human is constituted through basic exclusions, haunted by those figures that do not count in its tally. In effect, I am asking how the unequal distribution of grievability enters into and distorts our deliberate ways of thinking about violence and nonviolence. One might expect that a consideration of grievability pertains only to those who are dead, but my contention is that grievability is already operative in life, and that it is a characteristic attributed to living creatures, marking their value within a differential scheme of values and bearing directly on the question of whether or not they are treated equally and in a just way. To be grievable is to be interpellated in such a way that you know your life matters; that the loss of your life would matter; that your body is treated as one that should be able to live and thrive, whose precarity should be minimized, for which provisions for flourishing should be available. The presumption of equal grievability would be not only a conviction or attitude with which another person greets you, but a principle that organizes the social organization of health, food, shelter, employment, sexual life, and civic life.

In suggesting that violent potential emerges as a feature of all relations of interdependency and that a concept of the social bond that takes interdependency as a constitutive feature is one that perpetually reckons with forms of

ambivalence, I am accepting that conflict is an abiding potential, and one that is not overcome in any final way. I am less
interested in claiming that conflict is an intrinsic feature of
something called "the social bond" (as if there were a single
one) than in proposing that in considering specific social
relations, we can and should ask about the status of ambivalence in those relations, especially when those relations have
involved dependency—or interdependency. We may have
all sorts of other reasons for thinking about social relations,
but insofar as they are characterized by interdependency, it
becomes possible, in my view, to ask about *ambivalence* and
disavowal not only as features of an autonomous psychic
reality, but as *psychic features of social relations*—ones that
bear implications for understanding the problem of violence
within a relational frame, thus designating that convergence
as psycho-social.[16] Of course, that does not mean that we
think about violence only in that way, or even that it is the
best way. There are differences, between, say, physical, legal,
and institutional violence, that have to be understood. My
wager, in these chapters, is that we might gain some insight
into the way that demographic assumptions pervade our
debates about violence, especially when they take the form
of phantasmatic operations that motivate and disrupt delib-
erative efforts to think about violence in its justifiable and
unjustifiable instances.[17]

---

16 See Stephen Frosh, ed., *Psychosocial Imaginaries*, London: Palgrave,
2015.

17 Throughout this text, I follow the Kleinian practice of distinguishing fantasy, considered as a conscious state, analogous to a wish or daydream,
and phantasy, understood as an unconscious activity that operates through
projection and introjection and that blurs the boundary between affect

I have sought to show how equality, which now includes the idea of equal grievability, links to interdependency, and to the questions of why and how to practice nonviolence of a militant sort. One reason an *egalitarian approach to the value of life* is important is that it draws from ideals of radical democracy at the same time that it enters into ethical considerations about how best to practice nonviolence. The institutional life of violence will not be brought down by a prohibition, but only by a counter-institutional ethos and practice.[18]

Interdependency raises always that question of the destructiveness that is a potential part of any living relation. And yet, the social organization of violence and abandonment, traversing both the sovereign and biopolitical operations of power, constitutes the contemporary horizon in which we have to reflect upon the practice of nonviolence. The point bears repeating: if the practice remains restricted to an individual mode of life or decision making, we lose sight of that interdependency that alone articulates the

---

that emerges from within the subject and that which belongs to an object world. Although I do not seek to follow Klein in any rigorous way, I do want to suggest, for instance, that racial phantasms, however conscious they may be, are sustained by mechanisms of unconscious conversion of affect that equivocate between what belongs to oneself and what belongs to another. Although I do not accept a strict distinction between conscious and unconscious mental life, I do insist that social forms of power, like racism, can form subjects in unconscious ways, establishing deep and lethal patterns of the mind. See page 34 of this book for further discussion.

18   See Marc Crepon, *Murderous Consent*, trans. Michael Loriaux and Jacob Levi, New York: Fordham University Press, 2019; Adriana Cavarero and Angelo Scola, *Thou Shalt Not Kill: A Political and Theological Dialogue*, trans. Margaret Adams Groesbeck and Adam Sitze, New York: Fordham University Press, 2015.

relational character of equality, as well as of the possibility of destruction that is constitutive of social relations.

This leads me to a final point: the ethical stand of nonviolence has to be linked to a commitment to radical equality. And more specifically, the practice of nonviolence requires an opposition to biopolitical forms of racism and war logics that regularly distinguish lives worth safeguarding from those that are not—populations conceived as collateral damage, or as obstructions to policy and military aims. Further, we have to consider how a tacit war logic enters into the biopolitical management of populations: if the migrants come, they will destroy us, or they will destroy culture, or they will destroy Europe or the UK. This conviction then licenses violent destruction—or the slower death-in-life of detention camps—against the population that is phantasmatically construed as the locus of destruction. According to that war logic, it is a matter of choosing between the lives of refugees and the lives of those who claim the right to be defended against the refugees. In such instances, a racist and paranoid version of self-defense authorizes the destruction of another population.

As a result, the ethical and political practice of nonviolence can rely neither exclusively on the dyadic encounter, nor on the bolstering of a prohibition; it requires a political opposition to the biopolitical forms of racism and war logics that rely on phantasmagoric inversions that occlude the binding and interdependent character of the social bond. It requires, as well, an account of why, and under what conditions, the frameworks for understanding violence and nonviolence, or violence and self-defense, seem to invert into one another, causing confusion about how best to pin down those terms. Why is a petition for *peace* called a "violent" act? Why is a human barricade thwarting the police called an act of "violent" aggression? Under which conditions and within which frameworks does the inversion of violence and nonviolence occur? There is no way to practice nonviolence without first interpreting violence and nonviolence, especially in a world in which violence is increasingly justified in the name of security, nationalism, and neofascism. The state monopolizes violence by calling its critics "violent": we know this from Max Weber, Antonio Gramsci, and from Benjamin.[19] Hence, we should be wary about those who claim that violence is necessary to curb or check violence; those who praise the forces of law, including the police and the prisons, as the final arbiters. To oppose violence is to understand that violence does not always take the form of the blow; the institutional forms through which it operates compel us to ask: Whose life appears as a life, and whose loss would register as a loss? How does that demographic imaginary function in ethics, in policy, and in politics? If

---

19 See Weber's definition of the state as "a human community that (successfully) claims the monopoly of the legitimate use of physical force within a given territory." Max Weber, "Politics as a Vocation," in *From Max Weber: Essays in Sociology*, trans. H. H. Gerth and C. Wright Mills, Oxford, UK: Oxford University Press, 1946, 78. A more thorough analysis of violence and coercion would have to consider Gramsci's notion that class hegemony is maintained through coercion that functions as consent without the manifest threat of physical force. In the *Prison Notebooks*, for instance, he refers to what is required to facilitate a new mode of adaptation to a new mode of work, arguing that "pressure is exerted over the whole social sphere, a puritan ideology develops which gives to the intrinsic brutal coercion the external form of persuasion and consent." Antonio Gramsci, *Prison Notebooks, Volume One,* trans. Anthony Buttigieg, New York: Columbia University Press, 1992, 138.

we operate within the horizon in which violence cannot be identified, where lives vanish from the realm of the living before they are killed, we will not be able to think, to know, or to act in ways that embed the political in the ethical—that is, in ways that understand the claim of relational obligations within the global sphere. In a sense, we have to break open the horizon of this destructive imaginary in which so many inequalities and effacements now take place. We must fight those who are committed to destruction, without replicating their destructiveness. Understanding how to fight in this way is the task and the bind of a nonviolent ethics and politics.

In other words, we hardly need a new formulation of the state of nature, but we *do* need an altered state of perception, another imaginary, that would disorient us from the givens of the political present. Such an imaginary would help us find our way toward an ethical and political life in which aggression and sorrow do not immediately convert into violence, in which we might be able to endure the difficulty and the hostility of the social bonds we never chose. We do not have to love one another to be obligated to build a world in which all lives are sustainable. The right to persist can only be understood as a social right, as the subjective instance of a social and global obligation we bear toward one another. Interdependent, our persistence is relational, fragile, sometimes conflictual and unbearable, sometimes ecstatic and joyous. Many people say that arguing for nonviolence is unrealistic, but perhaps they are too enamored with reality. When I ask them whether they would want to live in a world in which no one was arguing for nonviolence, where no one held out for that impossibility, they always say no. The impossible world is the one that exists beyond the horizon of our present thinking—it is neither the horizon of terrible war, nor the ideal of a perfect peace. It is the open-ended struggle required to preserve our bonds against all that in the world which bears the potential to tear them apart. To subdue destruction is one of the most important affirmations of which we are capable in this world. It is the affirmation of this life, bound up with yours, and with the realm of the living: an affirmation caught up with a potential for destruction and its countervailing force.

To Preserve the Life of the Child

2

To Preserve the Life of the Other

I propose a relatively simple question, one that we might immediately identify as belonging to moral psychology, or perhaps to moral philosophy: What leads any of us to seek to preserve the life of the other? Of course, debates about the preservation of life now inform medical ethics, including those concerning reproductive freedom and technology, but also those regarding health care, law enforcement, and prisons. Although I will not be entering into those debates in detail here, I hope that some of what I argue will have implications for how we enter those debates. I want, rather, to point out a feature of debates about when and where the preservation of life is called for: namely, that we invariably make some assumptions about what counts as life. These assumptions include not only when and where it begins or how it ought to end, but also, perhaps in another register, the question of *whose lives* count as living.

So, when we ask the question, "Why do we seek to preserve the life of the other?" we could be asking about what motivates us to do so, or we could instead be asking what *justifies* actions of that kind—or, indeed, what establishes as morally unjustifiable the refusal or failure to preserve a life. The first question is psychological, though clearly one of moral psychology; the second belongs to moral philosophy, or to ethics, fields that sometimes rely on moral psychology to make their claims. But do these questions also overlap with social theory and political philosophy?

Much depends on how we pose the question and what assumptions we make when we pose it. For instance, it makes a difference if we pose the question about a singular other person: What leads any of us to seek to preserve the life of this other person? That question is different from asking whether we seek to preserve the lives of some particular group with which we strongly identify, those belonging to a vulnerable group that seems to us in danger of violence or destruction, or of all who are living. Asking what leads us to seek to preserve the life of a particular other person presumes a dyadic relation: You may be someone I know or someone I do not know; in either case, I may, under certain circumstances, be in a position to ward off danger or to stop a destructive force that threatens your life. What do I do, and why do I do it? And what justifies the action that I finally take? These questions seem to belong to the field of moral philosophy and moral psychology, without exhausting the range of questions considered by those fields. Asking whether we seek to preserve the life of some particular group— asking what justifies actions of that kind—presumes what we might well call a "biopolitical" consideration. It asks that we consider not only what counts as a life, but whose lives count as worthy of preservation. Under certain conditions, it makes sense to ask whose life *counts as a life*, even when that formulation seems to founder in tautology: if it is a life that does not count, is it not still a life?

I will return to this question of biopolitics in the next chapter. For now, let us return to the first question with which I began: What leads any of us to seek to preserve the life of the other? It is a question that, in some form, has to be asked not just of individuals, but also of institutional arrangements, economic systems, and forms of government: What structures and institutions are in place to safeguard the life of a population or, indeed, that of every population? We will turn to psychoanalysis to see what grounds are given there for *not* taking a life, and for seeking to preserve one. It is not a matter of thinking about the relation of individual to group psychology, for the two invariably overlap, and even our very singular and subjective dilemmas implicate us in a broader political world. The "I" and the "you," the "they" and the "we" are implicated in one another, and that implication is not only logical; it is lived out as an ambivalent social bond, one that constantly poses the ethical demand to negotiate aggression. So, if we start the moral inquiry with the uncritical use of the "I," or indeed the "we," we have occluded a prior and pertinent inquiry that considers how both the singular and plural subject are formed and contested by the relations they seek to negotiate through moral reflection.

The way this question is posed raises another: that of paternalism. Who belongs to the group who does the "preserving," and who is imagined as having lives in need of "preservation"? Are "we" not also in need of having our lives preserved? Are the lives of those who ask the question the same as the lives about whom the question is asked? For those of us who pose the question, do we consider that our own lives are also worthy of preservation, and if so, who is called upon to preserve them? Or is it rather that we presume the worthiness of our lives, presume that everything will be done to preserve our lives, such that "we" ask this question about "others" who do not live with such presumptions? Is the "we" really separable from those "other" lives we may seek to preserve? If there is a "we" who seeks to solve this problem, and then there are "others" who are the recipients of our deliberations, do we then assume a certain divide, arguably paternalistic, between those who have—or are invested with—the power to preserve life (or those of us for whom there exists a power that seeks already to preserve our lives) and those whose lives are in danger of not being preserved—that is, those whose lives are imperiled by a form of violence, either deliberate or negligent, and whose survival can only be countered by a countervailing sort of power?

This happens, for instance, when "vulnerable groups" are identified. On the one hand, the discourse on "vulnerable groups" or "vulnerable populations" has been important to both feminist human rights work and the ethics of care.[1] For

---

1   See Martha Fineman, "The Vulnerable Subject: Anchoring Equality in the Human Condition," *Yale Journal of Law and Feminism* 20:1, 2008; and Lourdes Peroni and Alexandra Timmer, "Vulnerable Groups: The Promise of an Emerging Concept in European Human Rights Convention Law," *International Journal of Constitutional Law* 11:4, 2013, 1056–85. See also Joan C. Tronto, *Moral Boundaries: A Political Argument for an Ethic of Care*, New York: Routledge, 1994; Tronto, *Caring Democracy: Markets, Equality, Justice*, New York: New York University Press, 2013; Daniel Engster, "Care Ethics, Dependency, and Vulnerability," *Ethics and Social Welfare* 13:2, 2019; and Fabienne Brugère, *Care Ethics: The Introduction of Care as Political Category*, Leuveb: Peeters, 2019.

if a group is called "vulnerable," then it gains a status that enables it to make a claim for protection. The question then emerges: To whom is that claim addressed, and which group emerges as charged with the protection of the vulnerable? On the other hand, have the ones who bear responsibility for vulnerable groups become divested of vulnerability through that designating practice? Of course, the point is to highlight the unequal distribution of vulnerability; but if such a designation implicitly distinguishes between vulnerable and invulnerable groups, and charges the invulnerable with the obligation to protect the vulnerable, then that formulation makes two problematic assumptions: first, it treats groups as if they are already constituted as vulnerable or not vulnerable; second, it fortifies a paternalistic form of power at the very moment in which reciprocal social obligations are most urgently required.

Those of us who understand ourselves as responding to an ethical claim to safeguard life, even to protect life, may find ourselves subscribing to a social hierarchy in which, for ostensibly moral reasons, the vulnerable are distinct from the paternalistically powerful. It is, of course, possible to claim that such a distinction is descriptively true, but when it becomes the basis of a moral reflection, then a social hierarchy is given a moral rationalization, and moral reasoning is pitted against the aspirational norm of a shared or reciprocal condition of equality. It would be awkward, if not fully paradoxical, if a politics based on vulnerability ended up fortifying hierarchies that most urgently need to be dismantled.

I began by posing a question about the psychological motivations for preserving another's life or the lives of others in the plural and sought to show that such a question, perhaps in spite of itself, opens onto a political problem concerning the management of demographic differences and the ethical ruses of paternalistic forms of power. As of yet, my inquiry leaves critically unexplored such key terms as "life," "the living," what it means "to preserve and to protect," and whether these can be thought as reciprocal actions such that those who potentially preserve the lives of others are also in potential need of preservation—as well as what that implies about potentially shared conditions of vulnerability and exposure, the obligations they imply, and the sorts of social and political organization they require.

My inquiry is meant to ask about the possibility of safe-guarding life against modes of destruction, including the kinds of destruction that we ourselves unleash. My wager is that not only do we find ways to preserve the very lives that we ourselves have the power to destroy, but also that such preservation of life requires infrastructures organized with that purpose in mind. (Of course, there are infrastructures that seek precisely not to preserve lives, so infrastructure alone is not a sufficient condition for the preservation of life.) My question is not just *what* we, as morally accountable subjects, do, or refuse to do, to preserve a life or set of lives, but *how* the world is built such that the infrastructural conditions for the preservation of life are reproduced and strengthened. Of course, in some sense, we do build that world; but, in another sense, we find ourselves emerging into a biosphere, including a built world, that we personally have never made. Further, as we know from the increasingly urgent issue of climate change, the environment changes as a result of human intervention, bearing the effects of our own powers to destroy the conditions of livability for human and non-human life-forms. This is yet another reason why a critique of anthropocentric individualism will turn out to be important to the development of an ethos of nonviolence in the context of an egalitarian imaginary.

An ethos of nonviolence, whatever that might prove to be, will turn out to be different from both moral philosophy and moral psychology, though moral inquiry takes us to a site where it opens up both psychoanalytic and political fields. When we take moral psychology as a point of departure, as Freud surely did when considering the origins of destructiveness and aggression, our reasoning makes sense only in light of fundamental political structures, including assumptions we make about how destructive potential inheres in any social bond. Of course, lives appear one way or the other only when viewed from specific historical perspectives; they acquire and lose value depending on the framework in which they are regarded, which is not to say that any given framework has the full power to decide the value of a life. The differential ways in which the value of life is gauged are informed by tacit schemes of valuation according to which lives are deemed to be more or less grievable; some achieve iconic dimensions—the absolutely and clearly grievable life—while others barely make a mark—the absolutely ungrievable, a loss that is no loss. And there is a vast domain of others whose value is foregrounded within one framework and lost within another, that is, whose value is flickering, at best. One could claim that there is a continuum of the grievable, but that framework does not let us understand those occasions in which, for instance, a life is at the same time actively mourned within one community and fully unmarked—and unmarkable—within a dominant national or international frame. And yet this happens all the time. It is one reason why the community that mourns also protests the fact that the life is considered ungrievable, not only by those responsible for taking the life, but also by those who live in a world where the presumption is that such lives are always vanishing, that this is simply the way things go. This is one reason why mourning can be protest, and the two must go together when losses are not yet publicly acknowledged and mourned. The mournful protest—and here we can think of Women in Black or the Abuelas de Plaza de Mayo in Argentina, or the families and friends of the Ayotzinapa forty-three[2]—makes the claim that this lost life ought not to have been lost, that it is grievable and should have been regarded as such long before any injury was done. And it demands the forensic evidence that will establish the story of the death and who is accountable. The failure of accounting for violent death makes it impossible to grieve. For though the loss is known, the explanation of how the death took place is not, and so the loss cannot be fully registered. The dead remain, to that extent, ungrievable.

One normative aspiration of this work is to contribute to the formulation of a political imaginary of the radical equality of grievability. It's not just that we all have a right to mourn the dead, or that the dead have the right to be mourned—that is doubtless true, but it does not capture the full sense of what I mean. There is a difference between someone's being grieved and that same person's bearing,

---

2 See Christy Thornton, "Chasing the Murderers of Ayotzinapa's 43," NACLA, September 17, 2018, nacla.org.

in their living being, a characteristic of grievability. The second involves the conditional tense: those who are grievable *would be* mourned if their lives *were* lost; the ungrievable are those whose loss would leave no trace, or perhaps barely a trace. So, if I were to call for "the radical equality of all those who *are* grievable," I would not be able to focus on the way that grievability is differentially allocated such that some do not rise to the level of the grievable, cannot be grasped as lives worth mourning. In the same way that we talk about the unequal distribution of goods or resources, I believe that we can also speak about the radically unequal distribution of grievability. That does not mean there is a center of power that distributes according to a calculus, but it may well mean that a calculation of this sort pervades regimes of power in more or less tacit ways. And though some may think that I am calling for everyone to cry in the face of another's death and to ask how we might grieve for those we do not even know, I want to suggest that grieving takes a different form, even an impersonal form, when the loss is not proximate, when it is loss at a distance or when, in fact, it is nameless. To say that a life is grievable is to claim that a life, even before it is lost, is, or will be, worthy of being grieved on the occasion of its loss; the life has value in relation to mortality. One treats a person differently if one brings the sense of the grievability of the other to one's ethical bearing toward the other. If an other's loss would register as a loss, would be marked and mourned, and if the prospect of loss is feared, and precautions are thus taken to safeguard that life from harm or destruction, then our very ability to value and safeguard a life depends upon an ongoing sense of its grievability—the conjectured future of a life as an indefinite potential that would be mourned were it cut short or lost.

The scenario I have offered acts as if the problem belongs to ethical relations structured in a dyadic way. I regard you as grievable and valuable, and perhaps you regard me as the same. Yet, the problem goes beyond the dyad and calls for a rethinking of social policy, institutions, and the organization of political life. Indeed, if institutions were structured according to a principle of the radical equality of grievability, that would mean that every life conceived within those institutional terms would be worth preserving, that its loss would be marked and lamented, and that this would be true not only of this or that life, but of every life. This would, I suggest, have implications for how we think about health care, imprisonment, war, occupation, and citizenship, all of which make distinctions between populations as more and less grievable.

And there is still that tricky question of life, and when life starts, and what kinds of living beings I have in mind when I speak about those who are "living": Are they subjects of a human kind? Would that include the embryonic, and so not quite a "they" at all? And what about insects, animals, and other living organisms—are these not all forms of living that deserve to be safeguarded against destruction? Are they distinct kinds of being, or are we referring to living processes or relations? What of lakes, glaciers, or trees? Surely they can be mourned, and they can, as material realities, conduct the work of mourning as well.[3]

---

3   See Karen Barad on the mourning of matter: Karen Barad, "Troubling Time/s and Ecologies of Nothingness: Re-turning, Re-membering, and Facing the Incalculable," *New Formations* 92, 2017.

For now, it seems worth reiterating that the ethic I am articulating is bound up with a specific political imaginary, an egalitarian imaginary that requires a conjectural way of proceeding, a way of experimenting with the conditional: only those lives that would be grieved if they were lost qualify as grievable lives, and these are lives actively and structurally protected from violence and destruction. This use of the grammatical form of the second conditional is one way of experimenting with a potential, postulating what would follow if all lives were regarded as grievable; it might let us see how a utopic horizon opens up in the midst of our consideration of whose lives matter and whose lives do not, or whose lives are more likely to be preserved and whose lives are not. Let us, in other words, embed our ethical reflections within an egalitarian imaginary. The imaginary life turns out to be an important part of this reflection, even a condition for the practice of nonviolence.

For the most part, when we confront moral dilemmas regarding the conditions under which life should be preserved, we formulate hypotheses and then test them by imagining various scenarios. If I were a Kantian, I might ask: If I act in a certain way, can I, without contradiction, will that everyone act in that same way, or at least in accord with the same moral precept? For Kant, the question is whether one commits a contradiction or acts reasonably in willing as one does. He gives us a negative and a positive formulation: "I ought never to act except in such a way that I can also will that my maxim should become a universal law";[4] and then,

---

4   Immanuel Kant, *The Moral Law: Groundwork of the Metaphysic of Morals*, trans. H. J. Paton, New York: Routledge, 1991, 73.

"Act always on that maxim whose universality as a law you can at the same time will."[5] One example he offers is that of the false promise, made to extricate oneself from a difficult situation. That route seems not to work, for "I become aware at once that I can indeed will to lie, but I can by no means will a universal law of lying."[6] Others, he claims, would "pay me back in like coin," and his "maxim, as soon as it was made a universal law, would be bound to annul itself."[7] I take it that I cannot reasonably will that false promising become a universal practice for the simple reason that I don't like the prospect of being lied to. Yet, I do have to imagine that very possibility if I am to understand the contradictory character of any maxim that permits of lying.

For consequentialists, of course, the imperative to imagine the consequences of living in a world in which everyone would act as you choose to act leads to the conclusion that some practices are utterly untenable, not because they are irrational, but because they inflict consequential damage that is unwanted. In both cases, I would suggest, a potential action is figured as hypothetically reciprocal: one's own act comes back in the imagined form of another's act; another might act on me as I would act on the other, and the consequences are unacceptable because of those damaging consequences. (For Kant, the damage is done to reason, though this is not the case for all moral philosophers who engage the hypothetical in that way.) The broader question is whether one would want to live in a world in which others acted

---

5   Ibid., 116.
6   Ibid., 75.
7   Ibid.

in the same way that I propose to act when I posit a set of violent acts. Again, we could conclude that it would be irrational to will something for myself that I could not possibly will for another. Or we might conclude that the world itself would not be livable if others were to act in the way that I propose to act, and then we would be indexing a threshold of livability.

In either moral experiment, one imagines one's act as someone else's, a potentially destructive act reversed or reciprocated. It is a difficult and disturbing kind of imagining, one that mandates my dispossession from my own act. The act that I imagine is no longer the one I imagine myself doing, even as it has something of me in it, to be sure; however, I have assigned it to a possible someone, or an infinite number of someones, and so have taken more than a bit of distance from the act itself. When the act returns, impressing itself upon me as the potential act of another, I should not really be surprised, since I started by distancing myself from the act that I aim to consider and attributing it to anyone and everyone. If the act is out there, the act of anyone, and it is thus not mine, then to whom does it finally belong? Thus, paranoia begins. My postulation is that such a form of imagining intersects with psychoanalysis and its account of fantasy in some important ways: one's action comes back to oneself in the form of another's action. That action might be duplicated or, in the case of aggression, be figured as emanating from the other and directed against oneself. In scenes of persecutory fantasy, the imagined return of one's own aggression through an external figure is hardly a livable situation. If we ask what links the act of imagining the reciprocated act in moral philosophy (how would it be if others acted as I act) and the reversals that take place in fantasy (whose aggression is it that comes back toward me in external form—could it be my own?), we may understand the act of imagining reciprocal action as crucial to an understanding of the ways in which one's own aggression becomes bound up with another's. This is not simply a mirror of projections or a cognitive misfire, but a way of thinking about aggression as part of any social bond. If the act that I imagine doing can, in principle, be the one that I also suffer, then there is no way to separate the reflection on individual conduct from the reciprocal relations that constitute social life. This postulation will turn out to be important for the argument I hope to make about the equal grievability of lives.

My suggestion is that the site where moral philosophy is quite radically implicated in psychoanalytic thought is the phantasmatic dimension of *substitutability*: the idea that one person can be substituted for another, and that this happens quite often in psychic life. Let me, then, briefly recast one version of a consequentialist view in light of this thesis: if I contemplate an action of destructiveness, and I imagine that others might do as I plan to do, I may end up casting myself as the recipient of that action. That might result in a persecutory fantasy (or phantasy in the Kleinian account which attributes to it an unconscious character) strong enough to dissuade me from acting as I thought (or surely wished) I might. The thought that others might do as I propose to do, or that others might do to me what I propose to do to others, proves to be unmanageable. Of course, if I become convinced that I will be persecuted, not realizing that the action I imagine is in part my own imagined action, carrying my own wish, then I might construct a rationale for acting aggressively against an aggression that is coming at me from the outside. I can use that persecutory phantasm as a justification for my own acts of persecution. Or it could, ideally, persuade me not to act, but only if I still recognize my own potential action in the phantasm that presses itself upon me.

That is all the more tragic or comic when one realizes that it is my own aggression that comes toward me in the form of the other's action and against which I now aggressively seek to defend myself. It is my action, but I assign it to another's name, and as misguided as that substitution may be, it nevertheless compels me to consider that what I do can be done to me. I say "consider," but this is not always a reflective procedure. Once a substitution becomes subject to fantasy, there are involuntary associations that follow. So though the experiment may start quite consciously, those kinds of substitutions, of me for another, of another for me, implicate me in an involuntary set of responses that suggest that the process of substitution, the psychic susceptibility to substitutability, a primary and transitive mimesis, cannot be fully orchestrated or restrained by a deliberate act of mind.[8] In some ways, substitution is prior to the very emergence of the "I" that I am, operating prior to any conscious deliberation.[9] So when

8 On primary mimesis, see Mikkel Borch-Jacobsen, *The Freudian Subject*, Stanford, CA: Stanford University Press, 1992; and François Roustang, *Qu'est-ce que l'hypnose?*, Paris: Éditions de Minuit, 1994.

9 Various versions of this thesis can be found in the work of Sándor Ferenczi, François Roustang, and Simon Critchley, for whom the relationship between Levinas and psychoanalysis proves central. See Adrienne Harris and Lewis Aron, eds., *The Legacy of Sándor Ferenczi: From Ghost to Ancestor*, New York: Routledge, 2015; and Simon Critchley, "The Original Traumatism: Levinas and Psychoanalysis," in Richard Kearney and Mark Dooley, eds., *Questioning Ethics*, New York: Routledge, 1999.

I consciously set myself the task of substituting others for me, or substituting myself for others, I may well become susceptible to an unconscious domain that undercuts the deliberate character of my experiment. Something is thus experimenting with me in the midst of my experiment; it is not fully under my control. This point will prove to be important to the question of why any of us should preserve the life of the other, since the question I pose reverses and expands in the course of its formulation, and is ultimately recast as a scene of reciprocal action. As a result, in seeing how my life and the life of the other can be substituted for one another, they seem to be not so fully separable. The links between us exceed any that I may have consciously chosen. It may be that the act of hypothetical substitution of myself for another, or another for me, brings us to a broader consideration of the reciprocal damage done by violence, the violence, as it were, done to reciprocal social relations themselves. And yet, sometimes this very capacity for substituting oneself for another and another for oneself can build up a world that leads to greater violence. How and why is this the case?

One reason we cannot, or may not, take away the lives of those we would rather see gone is that we cannot consistently live in a world in which everyone does the same. To apply this measure to our actions means that we have to imagine a world in which we *do* act that way, to set ourselves on the road to action and query whether there are grounds to stop ourselves. We have to imagine the consequences of our murderous action, and that involves passing through a disturbing fantasy, one that, I would suggest, is not altogether consciously orchestrated. For, to imagine that the other might die because of me suggests already that the reverse might be true: I might die at the hands of the other. And yet I may well compartmentalize my beliefs so that I imagine my action as unilateral and unreciprocated, which would mean that I become split off from entertaining the possibility of dying at the hands of the other. If one's beliefs are founded on such a denial, or such a splitting off, what consequences does that have for how one understands oneself?

In performing the thought experiment, one might conclude that others would seek to destroy me, or that they surely will, at which point I may conclude that I am a fool if I do not destroy them first. Once the thought experiment gives way to those modal possibilities of persecution, the argumentation can work to support the decision to kill. But what is the basis of such a perception of others as intent on destroying me?

Freud was not at all convinced that reason has the power to order and constrain murderous wishes—a remark he made when the world was on the brink of another war. And we can see how a form of circular reasoning can function as an instrument of aggression, whether that aggression is desired or feared. Given the reality of destructive urges, Freud argued that ethical severity is surely required. At the same time, he wondered whether ethical severity could do the job. In *Civilization and Its Discontents*, Freud makes a joke that the ethical severity of the super-ego "does not trouble itself enough about the facts of the mental constitution of human beings" since, in his words, "the ego does not have unlimited mastery over the id."[10] Freud claims, as

---

10 Sigmund Freud, *Civilization and Its Discontents*, in *The Standard Edition of the Complete Psychological Works of Sigmund Freud*, trans. James Strachey, vol. 21, London: Hogarth Press, 1915, 108–9. Abbreviated "SE" in subsequent citations.

well, that the commandment "Love thy neighbor as thyself" "is the strongest defense against human aggressiveness and an excellent example of the unpsychological proceedings of the cultural super-ego."[11] Earlier, in his "Thoughts for the Times on War and Death" (1915), he writes that no matter how elaborate our rational commitments might be, "the very emphasis on the commandment 'thou shalt not kill' makes it certain that we spring from an endless series of generations of murderers, who had the lust for killing in their blood, as, perhaps, we ourselves have to-day." After disputing the developmental trajectory of civilization—as well as the false moral promise of white rule—he asserts an unconscious dimension of lives that traverses all cultures: "if in our unconscious impulses we daily and hourly get rid of anyone who stands in our way . . . our unconscious will murder even for trifles."[12] Freud points out that "we may indeed wonder that evil should appear again so actively in persons who have received a [moral] education." Something about the murderous impulse remains to some degree uneducable, and this happens especially when individuals meld with groups.

We ought not to underestimate the power of this "unconquerable" dimension of psychic reality, one that he would come to associate with the death drive. Though we have focused briefly on the desire to kill, and even on what restrains us from killing, we can see that the death drive operates within political deliberations that are quite dissociated from the toll that they actually take on human life. We

---

11   Ibid., 109.
12   Sigmund Freud, "Thoughts for the Times on War and Death," SE vol. 14, 1914–16, 296–7.

might think about "collateral damage" as a prime instance of this kind of reasoning, one based on a disavowal that is, effectively, the instrument through which destruction happens.

We can find plenty of evidence of a resistance to legal and political forms of reciprocity: an insistence on the justification of colonial rule; a willingness to let others die through disease or lack of nutrition, or, perhaps, through closing the ports of Europe to newcomers and letting them drown, en masse, even though those bodies may well wash up on the shores of Europe's most coveted resorts. But there is, as well, sometimes a contagious sense of the uninhibited satisfactions of sadism, as we have seen in police actions against black communities in the United States in which unarmed black men running away from police are shot down with ease, and with moral impunity and satisfaction, as if those killed were hunted prey. Or, again, in the stubborn arguments against climate change by those who understand that by admitting to its reality, they would be obliged to limit the expansion of industry and the market economy. They know that destruction is happening, but prefer not to know, and in this way they arrange not to give a damn whether or not it happens as long as they make a profit during their time. In such a case, destructiveness happens by default; even if it is never said or thought, there is an "I don't give a damn about destruction" that gives license to destruction and perhaps even a sense of satisfactory liberation in opposing checks on industrial pollution and market expansion. We see, as well, in our contemporary political life how many people thrill to the various ways that Donald Trump calls for the lifting of prohibitions against racist policy and action, against violence—standing, it seems, for the liberation of the populace from the cruel and weakening super-ego, represented by the left and including its feminist, queer, and anti-racist proponents of nonviolence.

No position against violence can afford to be naive: it has to take seriously the destructive potential that is a constitutive part of social relations, or what some call "the social bond." But, if we take seriously the death drive, or that late version of the death drive defined as both aggression and destructiveness, then we have to consider more generally the kind of dilemma a moral precept against destruction poses for psychic life. Is this a moral precept that seeks to do away with a constitutive dimension of the psyche? And if it cannot do that, does it have another option besides strengthening the super-ego and its severe and cruel demands of renunciation? One Freudian response to this question is that the renunciation of such impulses is the best we can hope for, though we pay the psychic cost, of course, with a form of morality that now unleashes cruelty on our own impulses; its dictum might be understood this way: "Murder your own murderous impulse." Freud develops the idea of conscience in *Civilization and Its Discontents* along these lines, showing that destructiveness is now directed against destructiveness itself, and that because it cannot fully destroy its own destructiveness, it can intensify its operation as a super-egoic unleashing. The more intensely the super-ego seeks to renounce the murderous impulse, the more cruel the psychic mechanism becomes. At such a moment, aggression, even violence, is prohibited; but surely it is neither destroyed nor done away with, since it retains an active life lambasting the ego. This does not remain Freud's only way of handling destruction, as we shall see in Chapter 4 when we consider how ambivalence offers a pathway for ethical struggle.

In a sense, Freud is asking a similar question to the one I am posing here—What leads any of us to seek to preserve the life of the other?—but he is asking that question negatively: What, if anything, in psychic life keeps any of us from doing damage when we are in the grip of murderous wish? However, there is an alternative within psychoanalytic thinking, an affirmative way to rephrase that question: What kind of motivation is animated in psychic life when we actively seek to safeguard the life of another? Returning to the problem of substitution, we can ask: How do unconscious forms of substitution come to inform and vitalize what we might call "moral sentiments"? What conditions the possibility of putting oneself in the place of the other without precisely taking over that place? And what makes possible putting another in one's own place without precisely becoming engulfed? Such forms of substitution demonstrate the ways that lives are implicated in one another from the start, and this insight gives us a way to understand that whatever ethic we finally adopt, it won't do to distinguish between preserving oneself and preserving the other.

Melanie Klein makes a psychoanalytic contribution to moral philosophy in her essay "Love, Guilt, and Reparation," finding precisely in the dynamics of love and hate the site where individual and social psychology converge. Klein maintains that the desire to make people happy is linked with "strong feelings of responsibility and concern" and that "genuine sympathy with other people" involves "putting ourselves in the place of other people." To do this, "identification" brings us as close as we can get to the possibility of altruism: she writes, "We are only able to disregard or to some extent sacrifice our own feelings and desires, and thus for a time to put the other person's feelings and desires first, if we have the capacity to identify ourselves with the loved person." This disposition is not a full self-abnegation, for in seeking the happiness of the one we love we are understood to share in that person's satisfaction. A vicarious moment intervenes in the act of putting the other first, such that "we regain in one way what we have sacrificed in another."[13]

At this moment in her text, Klein drops down to a footnote that begins with the remark, "As I said at the beginning there is a constant interaction of love and hate in each of us."[14] Something about vicarious living brought on this reflection; or perhaps in order to conduct the discourse on love separately, it had to be graphically separated on the page from the discourse on aggression. In any case, the two discourses come funneling back to converge a few paragraphs on. In the footnote, she remarks that although she is now focusing on love in the text, she wants to make clear that aggression is co-present, that both aggression and hatred can be productive, and that we should not be surprised to find that people very capable of loving can and do also manifest these other feelings. She makes clear that in giving to others, and even in protecting them, we reenact the ways in which we have ourselves been treated by parents, or we reenact the phantasy about how we wish we had been treated. She keeps these

---

13   Melanie Klein and Joan Riviere, "Love, Guilt, and Reparation," in Melanie Klein and Joan Riviere, *Love, Hate, and Reparation*, New York: Norton, 1964, 66.

14   Ibid., 66, note 1.

two options open. She writes, "Ultimately, in making sacrifices for somebody we love and in identifying ourselves with the loved person, we play the part of the good parent, and behave towards this person as we felt at times the parents did to us—or as we wanted them to do."

So, though she has told us that "genuine sympathy" with another is possible and that it involves "the ability to understand them, as they are and as they feel," it is established through modes of identification that involve playing a role, even replaying a role, within a phantasmatic scene in which one is positioned as the child or as the parent, as they were or as they should have been, which is the same as what one "wished they were." In fact, Klein goes on to assert that "at the same time, we also play the part of the good child towards his parents, which we wished to do in the past, and are now acting out in the present."[15] So, let us note that in the moment of what Klein identifies as vicarious identifying essential to the effort to make another happy and even to give moral priority to that person over ourselves, we are role-playing and reenacting some unmourned losses or some unfulfilled wishes. She concludes the discussion this way: "By reversing a situation, namely, in acting towards another person as a good parent, in phantasy we re-create and enjoy the wished-for love and goodness of our parents."

At this point, it is unclear whether we had that good love and then lost it when we became older, or whether we only wished for that good love that we did not really have (or, at least, that did not fully fulfill our wishes). It seems now to matter whether in our vicarious and giving modalities we are

---

15   Ibid., 67.

actually mourning what we once had, or are instead wishing for a past we never had—or even experiencing a bit of both. At the point where Klein imports the discussion of aggression from the footnotes back into the text itself, she writes:

> But to act as good parents towards other people may also be a way of dealing with the frustrations and sufferings of the past. Our grievances against our parents for having frustrated us, together with the feelings of hate and revenge to which these have given rise in us, and again, the feelings of guilt and despair arising out of this hate and revenge because we have injured the parents whom at the same time we loved—all these, in phantasy, we may undo in retrospect (taking away some of the grounds for hatred), by playing at the same time the parts of loving parents and loving children.[16]

Thus, a discussion that begins with the assertion that genuine sympathy is possible through modes of identification develops into an exposition of how in treating others well and seeking to secure their happiness, we, each of us, replay our grievances against those who did not love us well enough or whose good love we have unacceptably lost.

At the same time, according to this logic, one is able now to be the good child one was not, or, rather, could not have been, given the waves of aggression that overwhelmed all those early efforts to be good. So I am, as it were, working out my losses and grievances, even expiating my guilt, when I engage in what Klein calls "genuine sympathy." I put the other first,

---

16   Ibid.

but my scene establishes all the roles that I or you can play. Perhaps it is all quite easy. I am only sharing in the satisfaction that I give the other because I love the other, and because what the other feels, I feel as well: genuine sympathy is possible and feeling is reciprocal. The simplicity of that formulation becomes questionable, however, once we ask whether the other to whom I give my love is ever encountered apart from those scenarios that I replay: my effort to reconstitute what I have lost, or what I never had; or my reconciliation of the guilt I have accrued in having sought, or seeking still, to destroy the other, even if only in phantasy. Is my sympathy motivated by my own loss and guilt, or is it the case that in sharing the other's happiness that I help to bring about, the "I" and the "you" are not as distinct as we might have thought? If they are sharing, what precisely do they share? Or are they partially obscured by the phantasy within which they appear?

When Klein concludes this discussion by claiming that "making reparation" is fundamental to love, she gives us another way to think about sympathy. Even as I have sympathy for another, perhaps for the reparation that another never received for a loss or for a deprivation, it seems that I am, at the same time, making reparation for what I never had, or for how I should have been cared for. In other words, I move toward the other, but I repair myself, and neither one of these motions takes place without the other. If identification involves playing out my losses, to what extent can it serve as the basis for a "genuine" sympathy? Is there always something "ungenuine" in the effort to make another happy, something self-preoccupied? And does this mean as well that identification with another is never quite successful if one condition of its possibility is a phantasy of self-reparation?

In these passages, Klein comes to focus on grievance and guilt, but grievance makes sense only in light of the claim that one has been deprived in the past. The deprivation may come in the form of loss (I once had that love and no longer do), or it may come in the form of reproach (I never had that love, and surely I should have had such love). Guilt in these passages seems to be linked with feelings of hatred and aggression. Whether or not one literally tore at, or tore apart, the parent, the phantasy is operative, and the child does not always know whether it was a phantasy of destruction or an actual deed. The continuing presence of the targeted parent does not suffice as living proof that the child is not a murderer, nor apparently does abundant documentation that the deceased parent died by natural causes. For the child, there is this murdered person living on in a more or less inexplicable way, sometimes under the same roof, or sometimes the child is the murdered person inexplicably living on (Kafka's Odradek in "The Cares of a Family Man"). Indeed, we cannot understand the reparative trajectory of identification without first understanding the way that sympathetic identification, according to Klein, is wrought from efforts to replay and reverse scenes of loss, deprivation, and the kind of hatred that follows from non-negotiable dependency.

Klein writes, "My psycho-analytic work has convinced me that when in the baby's mind the conflicts between love and hate arise, and the fears of losing the loved one become active, a very important step is made in development."[17] At issue is the fact that the phantasy of destroying the mother begets the fear of losing the very one on whom the infant

---

17   Ibid., 65.

is fundamentally dependent. To do away with the mother would be to imperil the conditions of one's own existence. The two lives seem to be bound together: "There is . . . in the unconscious mind a tendency to give her up, which is counteracted by the urgent desire to keep her forever."[18] The baby is no calculating creature. There is at some primary level a recognition that one's own life is bound up with this other life, and though this dependency changes form, I would suggest that this is the psychoanalytic basis for a theory of the social bond. If we seek to preserve each other's life, this is not only because it is in my interest to do so or because I have wagered that it will bring about better consequences for me. Rather, it is because we are already tied together in a social bond that precedes and makes possible both of our lives. My life is not altogether separable from the other life, and this is one way that phantasy is implicated in social life.

Guilt has to be understood not only as a way of checking one's own destructiveness, but as a mechanism for safeguarding the life of the other, one that emerges from our own need and dependency, from a sense that this life is not a life without another life. Indeed, when it turns into a safeguarding action, I am not sure it should still be called "guilt." If we do still use that term, we could conclude that "guilt" is strangely generative or that its productive form is reparation; but "safeguarding" is yet another future-directed modality, a kind of anticipatory care or way of looking out for another life that actively seeks to preempt the damage we might cause or that can be caused by others. Of course, reparation is not strictly tied to what has happened in the

18   Ibid., 91.

past: it might be undertaken for a damage I only *wished* to inflict, but never did. But "safeguarding" seems to do something else, establishing conditions for the possibility of a life to become livable, perhaps even to flourish. In this sense, safeguarding is not quite the same as preserving, though the former presupposes the latter: preserving seeks to secure the life that already is; safeguarding secures and reproduces the conditions of becoming, of living, of futurity, where the content of that life, that living, can be neither prescribed nor predicted, and where self-determination emerges as a potential.

Klein famously and repeatedly tells us that the infant feels great gratification at the mother's breast, but also great urges of destructiveness. In the presence of its own aggressive wishes, the infant fears that it has "destroyed the object which, as we know, is the one whom he loves and needs most, and on whom he is entirely dependent."[19] At another moment, the infant is said to feel not only guilt about losing the mother, or the one on whom he is most dependent, but also "distress," indicating an anxiety that belongs to a felt sense of radical helplessness.

"In the last analysis," she writes, "it is the fear that the loved person—to begin with, the mother—may die because of the injuries inflicted upon her in phantasy, which makes it unbearable to be dependent on this person."[20] This unbearable dependency nevertheless persists, delineating a social bond that, however unbearable, has to be preserved. Unbearable enough to give rise to a murderous rage, but one

---

19   Ibid., 61–2.
20   Ibid., 83.

that would, if acted out, given the dependency of one on the other, take down the both of them at once.[21]

Significantly, and perhaps paradoxically, the desire to give to the other, to make sacrifices for her, emerges from this recognition that if one destroys her, then one imperils one's own life. So, the child begins to repair the breach she understands herself to have instigated or imagined, or perhaps to repair the breach that is yet to come, thus countering destructiveness through repair. If I seek to repair her, I understand myself to have damaged her, or perhaps to have enacted a murder at a psychic level. In this way, I do not disavow my destructiveness, but I seek to reverse its damaging effects. It is not that destructiveness converts into repair, but that I repair even as I am driven by destructiveness, or precisely because I am so driven. Whatever sacrifices I make are part of the trajectory of reparation, and yet reparation is not an effective solution. Feminist literary theorist Jacqueline Rose notes that "reparation can reinforce omnipotence" and, moreover, that it sometimes emerges within Kleinian theory as a developmental, if not disciplinary, requirement and imperative.[22] Reparation is fallible and ought to be distinguished from efforts to rewrite, and so deny, the past. Such a form of hallucinatory denial may serve the purpose of dissociating from or reversing a psychic legacy of dependency and distress, producing a schizoid condition.

---

21 Lauren Berlant and Lee Edelman, *Sex, or the Unbearable*, Durham, NC: Duke University Press, 2013.

22 Jacqueline Rose, "Negativity in the Work of Melanie Klein," in *Why War?: Psychoanalysis, Politics, and the Return to Melanie Klein*, London: Blackwell, 1993, 144.

The psychoanalytic answer to the question of how to curb human destructiveness that we find in Freud focuses on conscience and guilt as instruments that re-circuit the death drive, holding the ego accountable for its deeds by means of a super-ego that lashes out with absolute moral imperatives, cruel punishments, and definitive judgments of failure. But this logic, in which one's destructive impulses are curbed through internalization, seems to find its culminating moment in a self-lacerating conscience or negative narcissism, as we saw in Freud.

In Klein, however, that inversion, or negative dialectic, spawns another possibility: the impulse to preserve that other life. Guilt turns out not to be fully self-referential, but one way to preserve a relation to another. In other words, guilt can no longer be understood as a form of negative narcissism that cuts the social tie, but rather as the occasion for the articulation of that very bond. Klein thus gives us a way to understand the important way that guilt marshals the destructive impulse for the purpose of preserving the other and myself, an act that presupposes that one life is not thinkable without the other. For Klein, this inability to destroy the one life without destroying the other operates at the level of phantasy. Although the developmental account presumes infant and mother, can we say that *this ambivalent form of the social bond takes a more general form once the interdiction against murder becomes an organizing principle of a sociality?* After all, that primary condition in which survival is insured through an always partially intolerable dependency does not exactly leave us as we age; indeed, it often becomes more emphatic as we age and enter into new forms of dependency that recall the primary ones, for instance, housing and institutional arrangements accompanied by caregivers, if they exist.

We saw, in the consequentialist scenario, how each of us concludes that it is really not in our best interest to go about killing those for whom we feel antipathy or emotional ambivalence, because then, others who feel antipathy toward us may well get the idea and decide to take our life or the life of another, since we would not be able to universalize any rule governing that mode of conduct without jeopardizing the very rationality that distinguishes us as humans and that constitutes the world as habitable. In different ways, each of these positions elaborates a scenario in which we are asked to duplicate or replicate our actions, imagining others in our position or projecting ourselves into the position of others, and then to consider and evaluate the action we propose to ourselves in light of that experiment. For Klein, however, we are from the start, and quite without deliberation, in a situation of substituting ourselves for another, or finding ourselves as substitutes. And that reverberates throughout adult life: I love you, but you are already me, carrying the burden of my unrepaired past, my deprivation and my destructiveness. And I am doubtless that for you, taking the brunt of punishment for what you never received; we are for one another already faulty substitutions for irreversible pasts, neither one of us ever really getting past the desire to repair what cannot be repaired. And yet here we are, hopefully sharing a decent glass of wine.

"Life, as we find it," Freud tells us in *Civilization and Its Discontents*, "is too hard for us."[23] This explains the need

---

23   Sigmund Freud, *Civilization and Its Discontents*, SE vol. 21, 1930.

for various forms of narcosis (including, of course, art). Carrying the burden of ungrievable loss, intolerable dependency, and irreparable deprivation, we seem to be, in what we call our "relations," spinning out scenarios of need for repair and seeking to repair through various forms of giving. It is, perhaps, a persistent dynamic, one in which polarities such as giving and receiving, or safeguarding and repairing, are not always distinct: who is acting is not always separable from who is acted upon. Perhaps this kind of morally and sensuously fecund ambiguity constitutes us in a potentially common way.

If my continuing existence depends upon another, then I am here, separated from the one on whom I depend, but also, quite crucially, over there; I am ambiguously located here and there, whether in feeding or in sleeping or in being touched or held. In other words, the separateness of the infant is in some ways a fact, but in significant ways it is a struggle, a negotiation, if not a relational bind. No matter how good the parenting, there is always some measure of distress and lack of gratification, since that other body cannot be there at every possible moment. So, hatred for the ones upon whom one is intolerably dependent is surely part of what is signified by the destructiveness that invariably surges forth in relations of love.

How, then, does this translate into a more general principle, one that might lead us back to the question of what keeps us from killing and what leads us to preserve the life of the other? Could it be that even now, in destroying another, we are also destroying ourselves? If so, it is because this "I" that I am has only ever been ambiguously differentiated, and is one for whom differentiation is a perpetual struggle and problem.

Klein and Hegel seem to converge here: I encounter you, but I encounter myself there, as you, reduplicated in my disrepair; and I myself am not just me, but a specter I receive from you searching for a different history than the one you had.

Thus, the "I" lives in a world in which dependency can be eradicated only through self-eradication. Some abiding truth of infantile life continues to inform our political lives, as well as the forms of dissociation and deflection out of which phantasies of sovereign self-sufficiency are born.[24] This is one reason, Rose has suggested, that if we want to avoid going to war, we should "hang on" to forms of "derision" and "failure" that preempt or undercut forms of triumphalism.[25]

We may think that a "genuine" sympathy requires that I understand myself as quite separate from you; but it may be that my capacity *not* to be me—that is, to play the role, even to act out the place of the other—is part of who I am, even what allows me to sympathize with you; and this means that in identification, I am partly comported beyond myself in you, and that what you levy in my direction is carried by me. So, there is some way in which we are lodged in one another. I am not only the precipitate of all those I have loved and lost, but also the legacy of all those who failed to love me well, as well as that of all the ones I imagine to have successfully kept me away from that intolerably early distress over my survival and away from that unbearable guilt (and anxiety) over the

---

24 At one point, Klein remarks that the infant's relation to the mother is the relation to life. She does not say, however, that it is the relation to the mother's life or to its own life. At that point, "life" is precisely a function of that ambiguous referent. Its own life, the life of the other; both are called "life."

25 Rose, "Negativity," 37.

destructive potential of my rage. And I endeavor to become the one who seeks to secure the conditions of your life and to survive whatever rage you feel about a dependency you cannot flee. Indeed, we all live, more or less, with a rage over a dependency from which we cannot free ourselves without freeing the conditions of social and psychic life itself.

But if we can imagine this dependency within personal life and intimate forms of dependency, can we not also understand that we are dependent on institutions and economies without which we cannot persist as the creatures that we are? Further, how might this perspective work to think about war, political violence, or the abandonment of populations to disease or to death? Perhaps the moral precept that prohibits killing has to be expanded to a political principle that seeks to safeguard lives through institutional and economic means, and to do so in a way that *fails* to distinguish between populations that are immanently grievable and those that are not.

In the next chapter, I hope to show that a consistent and expansive conception of a grievable life promises to revise our notions of equality in the spheres of biopolitics and the logics of war. The point is not only to find ways to repair the damage we have done (though that is surely important), or even the damage we believe we have done, but to anticipate and forestall the damage that is *yet to come*. For that purpose, an anticipatory form of repair has to be mobilized, an active form of safeguarding existing life for its unknowable future.[26] We might say: without that open future, a life

---

26   David Eng, "Reparations and the Human," *Columbia Journal of Gender and Law* 21:2, 2011.

is merely existing, but it is not living. My wager is that the reason we sometimes do not act violently is not simply that we calculate that someone else might act violently against us, and thus that it is not in our best self-interest to bring about that scenario. The reason, rather, is to be found in those conflicted social conditions that lay the ground for subject formation within the world of pronouns: this "I" that I am is already social, already bound to a social world that exceeds the domain of familiarity, both urgent and largely impersonal. I first become thinkable in the mind of the other, as "you" or as a gendered pronoun, and that phantasmatic ideation gives birth to me as a social creature. The dependency that constitutes what I am prior to the emergence of any pronoun underscores the fact that I depend on the ones whose definition of me gives me form. My gratitude is doubtless mixed with some understandable rage. And yet, it is precisely here where ethics emerges, for I am bound to preserve those conflicted bonds without which I myself would not exist and would not be fully thinkable. Thus, the matter of working with conflict and negotiating ambivalence becomes paramount to keep rage from taking violent forms.

If all lives are considered equally grievable, then a new form of equality is introduced into the understanding social equality that bears on the governance of economic and institutional life, which would involve a wrestling with the destruction of which we ourselves are capable, a force against force. This would be different from protecting the vulnerable by strengthening forms of paternalistic power. After all, that strategy always arrives late and fails to address the differential production of vulnerability. But if a life is regarded as grievable from the outset, considered as life that could potentially be lost, and that such a loss would be mourned, then the world organized itself to forestall that loss and safeguard that life from harm and destruction. If all lives are apprehended through such an egalitarian imaginary, how would that change the conduct of actors across the political spectrum?

It is notoriously difficult to get the message across that those who are targeted or abandoned or condemned are also grievable: that their losses would, or will, matter, and that the failure to preserve them will be the occasion of immense regret and obligatory repair. What disposition, then, allows us to establish the anticipatory powers of regret and remorse such that our present and future actions might forestall a future we will come to lament? In Greek tragedy, lament seems to follow rage and is usually belated. But sometimes there is a chorus, some anonymous group of people gathering and chanting in the face of propulsive rage, who lament in advance, mourning as soon as they see it coming.[27]

---

27   See Nicole Loraux, *Mothers in Mourning*, trans. Corinne Pache, Ithaca, NY: Cornell University Press, 1998, 99–103; see also Athena Athanasiou, *Agonistic Mourning: Political Dissidence and the Women in Black*, Edinburgh: Edinburgh University Press, 2017.

3

The Ethics and Politics of Nonviolence

In the previous chapters, I sought to engage psychoanalysis with both moral philosophy and social theory, intimating that some of our ethical and political debates make tacit demographic presuppositions regarding who poses the moral question and about whom the moral question is posed. We cannot even pose the question "Whose lives are to be safeguarded?" without making some assumptions about whose lives are considered potentially grievable. For lives that do not count as potentially grievable stand very little chance of being safeguarded. My suggestion has been that psychoanalysis helps us to see how phantasms can function as uncritical dimensions of moral deliberations that claim to be rational. Now we turn to Michel Foucault and Frantz Fanon, and what we might call "population phantasms" and "racial phantasms," to understand the tacit, even unconscious, forms of racism that structure state and public discourse on violence and nonviolence. Étienne Balibar and Walter Benjamin, read together, give us a way to understand the multiple senses of "violence," and the complex rhythm in which the violence of the state or other regulatory powers name as "violent" that which opposes their own legitimacy, such that this naming practice becomes a way of furthering and dissimulating their own violence.

I have suggested that moral debates on nonviolence can take two significantly different forms. The first centers on the question of the grounds for not killing or destroying another, or others in the plural, and the second on the question of what obligations we have to preserve the life of the other or others. We can ask what stops us from killing, but we can also ask what motivates us to find moral or political pathways that actively seek, where possible, to preserve life. Whether we pose such questions about individual others, specific groups, or all possible others matters greatly, since what we take for granted about the nature of individuals and groups, and even the ideas of humanity that we invoke in such discussions—very often demographic assumptions, including phantasies, about who counts as a human—conditions our views regarding which lives are worth preserving and which lives are not, and what defines and limits our operative notions of humanity. Etymologically considered, demography is the study of the way that the people (*demos*) are written (*graphos*) or represented, and though it is sometimes associated with statistics, that is only one of the graphic means by which populations are discursively elaborated. By what graphic means would we distinguish between the grievable and the ungrievable?

Grievable Lives: An Equality of Incalculable Value

I have suggested that violent potential emerges as a feature of all relations of interdependency, and that a concept of the social bond that takes interdependency as a constitutive feature is one that perpetually reckons with forms of ambivalence, ones that Freud understood as emerging from the conflict between love and hate. I hope to suggest that to recognize the unequal distribution of the grievability of lives can and should transform our debates about both equality and violence. Indeed, a political defense of nonviolence does not make sense outside of a commitment to equality.

If and when a population is grievable, they can be acknowledged as a living population whose death would be grieved if that life were lost, meaning that such loss would be unacceptable, and even wrong—an occasion of shock and outrage. On the one hand, grievability is a characteristic attributed to a group of people (perhaps a population) by some group or community, or within the terms of a discourse, or within the terms of a policy or institution. That attribution can happen through many different media and with variable force; and it can also *fail* to happen, or happen only intermittently and inconsistently, depending on the context and on how that context shifts. But my point is that people can be grieved or bear the attribute of grievability only to the extent that loss can be acknowledged; and loss can be acknowledged only when the conditions of acknowledgment are established within a language, a media, a cultural and intersubjective field of some kind. Or, rather, it can be acknowledged even when cultural forces are working to deny that acknowledgment, but that requires a form of protest: one that can break apart the obligatory and melancholic norm of disavowal, activating the performative dimension of public grieving that seeks to expose the limits of the grievable and establish new terms of acknowledgment and resistance. This would be a form of militant grieving that breaks into the public sphere of appearance, inaugurating a new constellation of space and time.[1]

We might prefer to adopt a humanist framework and assert that everyone, regardless of race, religion, or origin, has a life that is grievable, and then to militate for an acceptance of that basic equality. We may want to insist that this is a descriptive claim, that all existing life is equally grievable. But, if we let that be the full extent of our description, we badly misrepresent present reality, in which radical inequalities abound. So, we should perhaps make a move that is, frankly, normative: to claim instead that every life *ought to be* grievable, thus positing a utopic horizon within which theory and description must work. If we want to argue that every life is inherently grievable and claim a natural or a priori value for all, such a descriptive claim already carries with it the normative one—that every life *should be* grievable—so there is a question of why we ask the descriptive claim to do that normative work. After all, we have to point out the radical discrepancy between what is and what ought to be; so let us keep them distinct, at least for these kinds of debates. After all, theorizing within the terms of the present,

---

1 See Douglas Crimp, "Mourning and Militancy," *October* 51, 1989, 3–18; see also Ann Cvetkovich, "AIDS Activism and the Oral History Archive," *Public Sentiments* 2:1, 2003.

the more appropriate descriptive claim is certainly not that all lives are equally grievable. So, let us move from what is to what ought to be, or at least start that movement, one that posits a utopic horizon for our work.[2]

Further, when one speaks about lives that are not equally grievable, one posits an ideal of equal grievability. There are at least two implications of this formulation that pose some critical problems. The first is that we have to ask whether there is a way to measure or calculate how much anyone is really grieved. How does one establish that one population is more grievable and that another is less? And are there degrees of grievability? Surely, it would be quite disturbing, if not fully counterproductive, to establish a calculus that could provide answers of this sort. So the only way to understand this claim that some are more grievable than others—that some are, within certain frames and under certain circumstances, safeguarded against danger, destitution, and death more tenaciously than others—is to say precisely (and with Derrida) that the incalculable value of a life is acknowledged in one setting but not in another; or that within the same setting (if we can identify the parameters for the setting), some are acknowledged as bearing incalculable value, while others are subject to a calculation. To be subject to a calculation is already to have entered the gray zone of the ungrievable. The second implication of the formulation that not all lives are treated as equally grievable is that we now have to revise our ideas of equality in order to take into account grievability as

---

2   See Drucilla Cornell, *The Imaginary Domain*, London: Routledge, 2016 [1995]. See also Cornelius Castoriadis, *The Imaginary Institution of Society*, Cambridge, MA: MIT Press, 1997.

a social attribute that ought to be subject to egalitarian standards. In other words, we are not yet speaking about equality if we have not yet spoken about equal grievability, or the equal attribution of grievability. Grievability is a defining feature of equality. Those whose grievability is not assumed are those who suffer inequality—unequal value.

Foucault and Fanon on the War Logics of Race

As I suggested in Chapter 2, when we say that a life is ungrievable, we are not only speaking about a life that is already over. Indeed, to live in the world as a grievable life is to know that one's death *would be* mourned. But also, it is to know that one's life will be safeguarded because of its value. This way of evaluating the unequal grievability of lives is part of biopolitics, and that means that we cannot always trace this form of inequality to a sovereign decision-making process. In the final chapter of his 1976 lecture course "*Society Must Be Defended*," Foucault elaborates on the emergence of the biopolitical field in the nineteenth century. There, we find that "the biopolitical" describes the operation of power over humans as living beings. Distinct from sovereign power, biopolitics, or biopower, appears to be a distinctively European formation. It operates through various technologies and methods for managing both life and death. For Foucault, this is a distinct kind of power, inasmuch as it is exercised over humans by virtue of their status as living beings—sometimes he calls that living status a "biological" status, though he does not tell us which version of biological science he has in mind. Foucault describes the biopolitical as a regulatory power to "make live" or to "let die" distinct populations, distinguished from the sovereign power to "make die" or to "let live."[3]

As in many instances in Foucault's work, power acts, but not from a sovereign center: rather, there are multiple agencies of power operating in a post-sovereign context to manage populations as living creatures, to manage their lives, to make them live or let them die. This form of biopower regulates, among other things, the very livability of life, determining the relative life potentials of populations. This sort of power is documented in mortality and natality rates that indicate forms of racism that belong to biopolitics.[4] It emerges as well in forms of pronatalism and "pro-life" positions that regularly privilege some sorts of life, or living tissue (e.g., the fetus), over others (e.g., teenage or adult women). Thus, the "pro-life" position is committed to inequality, and in that way continues and intensifies the social inequality of women and the differential grievability of lives.

Important for our purposes is Foucault's claim that there is no a priori right to life—that a right to life must first be established in order to be exercised. Under conditions of political sovereignty, for instance, a right to life—and even a right over one's own death—comes to exist only for those

---

3 Michel Foucault, "*Il Faut Défendre la Société,*" *Cours au Collège de France (1975–1976)*, Paris: Seuil, 1976, 213. "La souveraineté faisait mourir et laissait vivre. Et voilà que maintenant apparaît un pouvoir que j'appellerais de régularisation, qui consiste, au contraire, à faire vivre et à laisser mourir."

4 For Ruth Wilson Gilmore, "racism, specifically, is the state-sanctioned or extralegal production and exploitation of group-differentiated vulnerability to premature death." Ruth Wilson Gilmore, *Golden Gulag: Prisons, Surplus, Crisis, and Opposition in Globalizing California*, Berkeley: University of California Press, 2007, 28.

who have already been constituted as rights-bearing subjects. Under biopolitical conditions, however, the "right" to life is much more ambiguous, since power manages *populations* rather than distinct subjects. Additionally, the relation of the biopolitical to matters of life and death is different from what he calls "the relationships of war." War logics follow the dictum: "If you want to live, you must take lives, you must be able to kill."[5] He reformulates this basic maxim of war at least twice, and it appears subsequently as: "In order to live, the other must die." In the first version, you yourself have to be prepared to kill, and killing is a means to preserve your own life. In the second version, in order to live, the other must die, but you yourself do not have to be the one who takes that other life. This opens the way to other technologies and procedures by which lives can be abandoned or "let to die" without any *one* assuming responsibility for the action.[6]

The way race enters war, or, indeed, the way in which state racism enters into wars that operate through biopolitical logics, is more difficult to discern in this view. Foucault has separated the biopolitical from the idea of warfare to the extent that he claims that biopower has a different relation to death. He writes that in biopower, "death does not swoop down," but that life and death are regulated through other kinds of managerial and institutional logics. However, the days of death swooping down are not exactly over, even if

---

5　The "you"—the *on* in French—is ambiguously singular and plural, so it is unclear whether war follows from self-preservation or from group preservation. Foucault, "*Il Faut Défendre*," 255.

6　Ibid., 213.

sometimes Foucault writes as if they were, in order to foreground another kind of power. For him, power and violence are now more indirect, less spectacular, less orchestrated by state violence. But it is not so easy to separate sovereign power from the biopolitical—a point that he himself would make in subsequent lectures—and we should consider suspect any effort to establish a neat historical sequence in which one clearly follows upon the other. That is especially the case if the sequence depends on a progressive version of modern European history—one that, by the way, does not take account of European wars suffered and waged during the last two centuries.

What happens if a life is considered not to be living at all, that is to say, what happens if it does not register as a life? If Foucault could claim very clearly that a right to life belongs only to a subject who is already constituted as a rights-bearing subject, one for whom life is a necessary right, can we not also then claim that the status of a living being must first be constituted for someone to become a subject with the right to life? If racism is a way of "introducing a break into the domain of life that is under power's control," as he claims, then perhaps we can think of that break as distinguishing not merely between superior and inferior types within the idea of the species, but also between the living and the nonliving.[7] After all, if a nonliving population is destroyed, then nothing of note has happened: there is no

---

7   For Foucault, racism constitutes the biopolitical as a "caesura," or a rupture, within the species: "That is the first function of racism: to fragment, to create caesuras within the biological continuum addressed by biopower." Michel Foucault, *"Society Must Be Defended,"* trans. David Macey, New York: Picador, 2003, 255.

destruction, just a certain clearing away of some curious obstruction from the path of the living.

Foucault anticipates that critics from the field of political theory will ask about his account of life. He retreats from this debate, perhaps fearing that it would commit him to a vitalism or to a foundationalist account of life that precedes contract, sovereignty, and the biopolitical.[8] "All this is a debate within political philosophy that we can leave on one side," he writes, "but it clearly demonstrates how the problem of life came to be problematized within the field of political thought."[9] The issue cannot quite be set aside, but this is not because there are assumptions about the form of life that precede the domain of power. Rather, in my view, power is already operating through schemas of racism that persistently distinguish not only between lives that are more and less valuable, more and less grievable, but also between lives that register more or less emphatically as lives. A life can register as a life only within a schema that presents it as such. The epistemological nullification or foreclosure of the living character of a population—the very definition of a geno-cidal epistemology—structures the field of the living along a continuum that has concrete implications for the question: Whose are the lives that are worth preserving, whose lives matter, whose lives are grievable?

To ask the question is to confront from the start this particular "historic-racial schema"—a term prominently used by Frantz Fanon in *Black Skin, White Masks*—a

8   See Catherine Malabou, "One Life Only: Biological Resistance, Political Resistance," *Critical Inquiry* 42:3, 2016.

9   Ibid., 241.

schema that functions as a form of perception and projection, an interpretive casing that enfolds the black body and orchestrates its social negation. In fact, Fanon distinguishes between the historic-racial schema and the "racial-epidermal schema" (which fixes an essence to black life), but it is the first that seems to bear a direct relation to the French phenomenologist Maurice Merleau-Ponty's idea of a "corporeal schema" and to the schemas of racism that bear on grievability. A corporeal schema, for Merleau-Ponty, is the organization of tacit and structuring bodily relations with the world, but it is also the operation of constituting oneself within the terms made available by that world. The historic-racial schema, according to Fanon, is to be found at a deeper level, and it comes to disrupt the idealized corporeal schema proposed by Merleau-Ponty.[10] The elements of the historic-racial schema are provided by what he calls "the white man"—a figure for the powers of racism that cast black bodily experience of the world into "certain uncertainty." On the one hand, a "third-person consciousness" enters into a "first-person consciousness," so one's very mode of perception is riven by another consciousness. Who is seeing when I am seeing, and when I see myself, am I seeing only through the eyes of another? On the other hand, the corporeal schema describes ways of composing oneself from the elements of the world: Fanon describes this aspirational "schema" as "a slow composition of my self as a body in the middle of a spatial and temporal world." The powerful figure of what he calls "the white man" is the one "who had woven me out of a thousand details, anecdotes,

10   Frantz Fanon, *Black Skin, White Masks*, New York: Grove, 2008, 91.

and stories."[11] So, as he writes, he retells having been written or woven by the third person, and we see on the page the slow struggle of self-composition that follows upon the decomposition of the bodily schema through the working of racism. It is at the level of the bodily experience of oneself in a world, where that schema is taken apart, expropriated, inhabited, occupied, and decomposed.

Of course, Fanon uses the first and the third person, figures such as the black man and the white man, to articulate this idea of the schema. But the historic-racial schema is broader and more diffuse than those particular figures. In fact, such a schema bears upon the living and embodied life of populations and so provides a critical supplement to Foucault's reflections on anti-black racism and biopower. Such a historic-racial schema also precedes and informs policies on world health, hunger, refugees, migration, culture, occupation and other colonial practices, police violence, incarceration, the death penalty, intermittent bombardment and destruction, war, and genocide. Although Foucault identifies "state racism" at the end of these lectures as one of the central instruments for the management of the life and death of populations, he does not tell us precisely how racism works to establish relative values for different lives. There is, of course, a clear sense that some populations are targeted by modes of sovereign power and that there is a "letting die" orchestrated by biopower, but how do we account for the differential ways in which lives and deaths matter or fail to matter? If we take racialization as a process by which a racial schema is materialized in the very

---

11   Ibid.

perception of whose life matters and whose does not,[12] then we can proceed to ask: How do such differentiated modes of perception enter into military and policy debates regarding targeted populations and incarcerated peoples? And in what ways do they operate as a set of uncritically accepted presuppositions—racial schemas—in our own debates about violence and nonviolence?

At the close of *"Society Must Be Defended,"* Foucault opens up the possibility that populations who are precarious or abandoned are not yet constituted as subjects of rights, and that in order to understand who they are—that is to say, the way they are constituted within the political field—we need an alternative to the model of the subject. This opens a direction to think about state racism as well as the modes of agency and resistance that emerge from a population that can be described neither as an individual nor as a collective subject; but sadly, that direction did not end up being the path that Foucault would take.[13]

Perhaps that abandoned project might still be revived: if, as Foucault has argued, under sovereign power a subject has a right to life only on the condition that the subject is constituted as a rights-bearing subject, then under conditions of biopower, a population has a claim to life on the condition that that population is registered as potentially

12   See Michael Omi and Howard Winant, *Racial Formation in the United States*, 3rd ed., London: Routledge, 2015; and Karim Murji and John Solomos, eds., *Racialization: Studies in Theory and Practice*, Oxford, UK: Oxford University Press, 2005.

13   See Kim Su Rasmussen, "Foucault's Genealogy of Racism," *Theory, Culture, and Society* 28:5, 2011, 34–51; and Ann Stoler, *Race and the Education of Desire*, Durham, NC: Duke University Press, 1995.

grievable. That is my thesis, my way of offering a supplement to Foucault by bringing Fanon to bear on the question of how racial schemas enter into the racial figurations of what is living, of the racial phantasms that inform the demographic valuations of who is grievable and who is not, whose lives ought to be preserved and whose can be expunged or left to die. Of course, there is a vast continuum of grievability, and populations can be grieved in one context and remain unmarked in another; and some modes of grieving may be acknowledged while others are dismissed or go unrecognized. And still, the dominant schemas by which the value of life is allocated rely on a modulation of grievability, whether or not that metric is ever named.

The historic-racial schema that makes it possible to claim, "This is or was a life," or, "These are or were lives," is intimately bound up with the possibility of necessary modes of valuing life: memorialization, safeguarding, recognition, and the preservation of life. ("This is a life worth living, worth preserving"; and "These are lives that ought to be given the condition to live and to be registered and recognized as lives.") The phantasmagoria of racism is part of that racial schema.[14] We can see how it works as a thought sequence crystallized in the moving images that enter into deliberation processes to negate the life claim of the person whose life is at stake—how the phantasmagoria of racism operates

---

14   Both the racial-epidermal schema and the historic-racial schema are at work in this phantasmagoria. The attribution of an essence to a racial minority can be a way of negating the value of that life, but also of negating in advance the very possibility of apprehending that life as a life.

within the metric of grievability. It does so, for instance, in the sequence in which a person, such as Eric Garner in the United States in 2014, is put into a police choke hold, and then audibly announces he cannot breathe and visibly can be seen to be unable to breathe, and it is registered by everyone at the scene that he will not survive the prolongation of that police choke hold, which then, after the announcement, strengthens to become a stranglehold, strangulation, murder. Does the police officer who strengthens the hold to the point of death imagine that the person about to die is actually about to attack, or that their own life is endangered? Or is it simply that this life is one that can be snuffed out because it is not considered a life, never was a life, does not fit the norm of life that belongs to the racial schema; hence, because it does not register as a grievable life, a life worth preserving? Or when Walter Scott, in South Carolina in 2015, turned his back to the police, unarmed, clearly frightened, and ran in the opposite direction from them—how did he become phantasmagorically turned around, made into a threatening figure to be killed? Perhaps there, in the moment of decision or action that belongs to a race-war logic: the police person believes it is their own life, rather than the other's, that is endangered. And perhaps this is simply the violent moment of a biopolitical apparatus, a way of managing that life unto death. In that case, the black man is simply there, vulnerable to being killed, and so he is killed, as if he is prey and the police are hunters. Or consider Trayvon Martin, killed by George Zimmerman who was subsequently acquitted, but also Marissa Alexander, in that same district, who was sentenced to twenty years for attempting to defend herself against sexual assault.

So, when unarmed black men or women, or queer and transgendered people, have their backs turned to police and are walking or running away, and they are still gunned down by police—an action often defended later as self-defense, even as a defense of society—how are we to understand this? Is that turning of the head or walking or running away actually an aggressive advance anticipated by the police? The police person who decides to shoot, or who simply finds himself shooting, may or may not be deliberating; but it surely seems that a phantasm has seized upon that thought process, inverting the figures and the movements he sees to justify in advance any lethal action he may take. The violence that the policeman is about to do, the violence he then commits, has already moved toward him in a figure, a racialized ghost, condensing and inverting his own aggression, wielding his own aggression against himself, acting in advance of his own plans to act, and legitimating and elaborating, as if in a dream, his later argument of self-defense.

Of course, the frame for this violence has to be expanded to include forms of violence that target race and gender at once, and so to reveal that sometimes the violence against black women, in particular, takes place in different scenes, in different sequences of events, and with differing consequences. The report "Say Her Name: Resisting Police Brutality against Black Women," published in July 2015 by the Center for Intersectionality and Social Policy Studies, led by Kimberlé Williams Crenshaw and Andrea Ritchie, makes clear that nearly all of the main examples in the media illustrating police violence against black people in the United States involve black men, establishing that the dominant frames for understanding anti-black racism and police violence operate within a restrictive gender framing.[15] Calling for "a gender-inclusive approach to racial justice," Crenshaw has independently drawn attention to the way that black women are overpoliced and underprotected, but also to how their injuries and deaths are not as fully documented or registered, even within those social movements explicitly focused on opposing police violence.[16]

To bring that problem into visibility, we would have to account for the various ways that black women face death in their encounters with police, whether on the street, in their homes, or in detention. There are the women stopped for traffic violations who then end up shot: Gabriella Nevarez in Sacramento in 2014, or Shantel Davis in Brooklyn in 2012, or Malissa Williams in Ohio in 2012, or LaTanya Haggerty in Chicago in 1999. And then, of course, in July 2015, Sandra Bland was pulled over for failing to signal when changing lanes, charged with assault, and held in jail in Waller County, Texas, only to be found dead in her cell three days later. It remains unclear whether that was a suicide or a murder. Worth noting, as well, is the number of black women killed when police are called to intervene in domestic disputes—the police often claim the women were aggressive or wielding knives, which may or may not be true, but in some instances it seems that it is the failure to obey a police order that results in being shot. But it is not always a direct killing that takes a life: a call for a doctor to help

---

15 African American Policy Forum, "#SayHerName: Resisting Police Brutality against Black Women," AAPF official website, aapf.org.

16 Kimberlé Williams Crenshaw, "From Private Violence to Mass Incarceration," *UCLA Law Review* 59, 2012, 1418.

with asthma goes unanswered, and Sheneque Proctor dies in a prison cell in Bessemer, Alabama, in 2014. Overpoliced, black women are often figured as aggressive, dangerous, out of control, or drug mules; underprotected, their own calls for help often go unheeded or scorned, as do their calls for medical or psychiatric treatment.

Contemporary European racism perhaps takes different forms, but the efforts to block migrants to Europe are in part rooted in the desire to keep Europe white, to safeguard a nationality that is imagined to be pure. It hardly matters that Europe has never been exclusively white, since the idea of European whiteness is a fantasy that seeks to be realized at the expense of a living population that includes people from North Africa, Turkey, and the Middle East. If we follow Foucault on biopower, and read him together with Achille Mbembe on necropolitics,[17] then we can approach analytically the policies that reproduce this metric of grievability. The thousands of migrants who have lost their lives in the Mediterranean are precisely lives that are not deemed worthy of safeguarding. Those waters are monitored for the purposes of trade and maritime safety; there is often cell coverage. So, how many countries have to disavow responsibility in order for those people to be left to die? Even if we could track the decision not to send help to boats in distress to this or that functionary from a European government, we would not quite grasp the large-scale policy that effectively lets populations die, that would rather let them die than let

17 Achille Mbembe, "Necropolitics," *Public Culture* 15:1, 2003, 11–40; see also *Necropolitics*, Durham, NC: Duke University Press, 2019.

them in. On the one hand, these are decisions, and we can track who is accountable for deciding in this way; on the other hand, the metric of grievability is built into these decisions in such a way that migrant populations are ungrievable from the start. We cannot lose those who cannot be grieved. They are treated as beyond losing, already lost, never living, never having been entitled to life.

All of these forms of taking life or letting life die are not just concrete examples of how the metric of grievability works; they wield the power to determine and distribute the grievability and value of lives. These are the concrete operations of the metric itself, its technologies, its points of application. And in these instances, we see the convergence of the biopolitical logic of the historic-racial schema with the phantasmagoric inversions that occlude the social bond: what may appear as an isolated act of violence or as the expression of an individual psychopathology shows itself to be part of a pattern, a punctual moment within *a reiterated practice* of violence. That practice relies upon and consolidates a racial schema in which aggression becomes justified through a logic that draws upon the phantasmagoric inversion of aggression, functioning not only as a potential defense, but as the effective moralization of murder—a racial schema in which the living status of the migrant, who fails to be registered within the perceptual field of the grievable, is already snuffed out, because from the start, such a life was not worth safeguarding and did not register as a life.

Law's Violence: Benjamin, Cover, Balibar

We may conclude that a stronger and more just sense of law should be brought to bear on such instances. The notion, however, that conflicts should be handled through law rather than through violence presumes that law does not wield its own violence and that it does not redouble the violence of the crime. We cannot readily accept the idea that violence is overcome once we make the transition from an extra-legal violent conflict to the rule of law. As we know, there are fascist and racist legal regimes that immediately discount that view, since they have their own rule of law—one that we would, on extra-legal grounds, call "unjust." We could say that those are instances of bad law, or we could say that what those regimes offer is not really law, and then stipulate what law should be; but that route does not address whether the legally binding character of law requires and institutes coercion, or whether coercion is distinguishable from violence. If it is not, then the move from an extra-legal conflictual field to a legal field is a shift from one kind of violence to another.

Over and against the view that law establishes civil relations based on freedom and that war establishes coercive conditions for conduct, Walter Benjamin clearly identifies the coercion at the heart of legal regimes as violence (*Gewalt*), not only in their punitive and carceral power, but also in the very making and imposing of laws themselves. Not surprisingly, his essay "Critique of Violence" is often regarded as ending with the figure of divine power, understood as purely destructive anarchism. And yet, the text begins with a consideration of both the natural law of tradition and positive law, showing the limits of each. At the outset, the kind of critique he undertakes is described as "philosophic-historical," which means that he is trying to understand how certain modes of justification have become part of legal reasoning and its power. In particular, he focuses on the fact that when violence is debated within the terms of the legal tradition he is considering, it is almost always considered as a "means." A natural law theorist will ask whether violence serves a "just end," calling upon an idea of justice that is already decided. A positivist will claim that it is not possible to justify an end outside of a legal system's own terms, since the law is what furnishes our ideas of justice. In either case, violence is approached first through the question: What justifies violence, or in light of what end is violence justified? This leaves open the question of whether we can know violence outside of the justificatory schemes by which it is approached. That approach figures the object in advance, so how might we then know violence, apart from those schemes? And if those schemes furnish justifications for the violence of a legal system and regime as distinct from any counter-violence (which would be unjustified), then to what extent must we set aside those modes of justification in order to grasp the larger picture, one in which states and legal powers justify their own violence as legitimate coercion and cast all forms of counter-violence as unacceptable violence?

In fact, Benjamin offers three interrelated forms of violence in this essay, distinguishing between "law-instating" (*rechtsetzend*) and "law-preserving" (*rechtserhaltend*) violence, and later introducing "divine violence" (*göttliche Gewalt*). Generally speaking, law-preserving violence is exercised by the courts and, indeed, by the police, and it represents the repeated and institutionalized efforts to assert and apply existing law such that it remains binding on the population it governs. Law-instating violence is the making of new law, for instance, law that is established when a polity comes into being. For Benjamin, no deliberation within the state of nature gives rise to law; law comes into being through retribution or the exercise of power. In fact, law making is a prerogative exercised by the military or the police when either initiates coercive actions to handle a population considered unruly or threatening. In his view, the acts by which law is posited, brought into being, are the work of "fate." Laws instituted in this way are justified neither by prior law nor through recourse to a rational justification or a rational set of ends. Rather, the justifications for law always postdate the law itself. Law does not, then, form organically over time, codifying existing conventions or norms. Rather, the instituting of law is what first creates the conditions for justificatory procedures and deliberations over justifiable actions to take place. Law is, in other words, the implicit or explicit framework in which we consider whether or not violence is a justified means for achieving a given end, but also whether a given force should be called "violent" or not. The legal regime, once founded, also establishes justificatory schemes and naming practices. In fact, it does this through fiat, and this is part of what is meant by the violence of founding the law. In effect, the violence of law-instating violence is there in the binding imperative with which it begins: "This will be law," or "This is now the law." The continuity of a legal regime requires the reiteration of the binding character of the law, and to the extent that police or military powers assert the law, they not only recapitulate the founding gesture ("This will be law") but also preserve the law. Although law-instating and law-preserving *Gewalt* are described by Benjamin as distinct, the police operate both forms, which implies that the law is "preserved" only by being asserted, again and again, as binding. The law thus depends on the police or the military to assert and preserve the law.

To the extent that Benjamin seeks to describe this operation of violence in the law, he seeks to establish a critical position on legal violence. Although many readers move directly to his invocation of "divine violence" at the end of the essay, it is largely misread, and that swift move toward what is most incendiary tends to overlook a section of the text that opens up the possibility of nonviolence. In fact, the only time that Benjamin explicitly names "nonviolence" in that text is in relation to what he calls "nonviolent conflict resolution," which takes form as a "technique of civil governance." This technique is, importantly, not a means designed to achieve an end. Nonviolence is not a means to a goal nor is it a goal in itself. It is, rather, a technique that exceeds both an instrumental logic and any teleological scheme of development—it is an ungoverned technique, arguably ungovernable. It is ongoing, open ended, and, therefore, what he calls "a pure means"—another name for his developing notion of critique as an active mode of thought or understanding, unconstrained by instrumental and teleological logics. If, theoretically, Benjamin is seeking to query the limits of those justificatory schemes established by legal violence and serving its aims, then the technique of conflict resolution is a practice that operates outside such logic, escaping its violence and enacting a nonviolent alternative.

Against the Hobbesian understanding of the contract as a way of resolving "natural" (pre-legal) violent conflict, Benjamin insists, in "Critique of Violence," that "a totally nonviolent resolution of conflicts can never lead to a legal contract," since, for him, the contract is the beginning of legal violence.[18] Later in the essay, he takes a next step: "There is a sphere of human agreement that is nonviolent to the extent that it is wholly inaccessible to violence: the proper sphere of 'understanding,' language [*die eigentliche Sphäre der 'Verständigung,' die Sprache*]."[19] What account of language is this, in which it is at once synonymous with "understanding" and "nonviolence"? And how does it illuminate what Benjamin comes to say about divine violence, which, if anything, seems overwhelmingly destructive?

Written in 1921, at roughly the same time, Benjamin's "The Task of the Translator" seems indirectly referenced here. In that text, Benjamin does not refer to "violence" and "nonviolence," but he does foreground the power of translation to enhance and augment communicability, suggesting that it can ameliorate impasses in communication.[20] Does translation relate, then, to the technique of conflict resolution? For one, translation seeks to overcome the situation of "non-communicability" imposed by distinct natural or

18 Walter Benjamin, "Critique of Violence," in *Walter Benjamin: Selected Writings, Volume 1: 1913–1926*, eds. Marcus Bullock and Michael W. Jennings, Cambridge, MA: Harvard University Press, 2004, 243.

19 Ibid., 245 and 248.

20 Benjamin, "The Task of the Translator," in *Walter Benjamin: Selected Writings, Volume 1*, 260–62. See also "On the Program of the Coming Philosophy" (1918) in *Selected Writings, Volume 1*, where the continuous development of communicability conditions the relation between philosophy and religion (100–13).

sensuous languages. Further, translation from one text to another helps to develop and further realize an ideal intrinsic to language: "language as such," one that overcomes impasse and the failure of communication and the impossibility of contact. In his 1916 essay "On Language as Such and the Languages of Man," Benjamin insists it is "the divine name" that moves past communicative impasse, which he specifies as "the divine infinity of the pure word."[21] In "The Task of the Translator," subsequently, the non-sensuous "intention" that runs through all languages is named the "divine word." This does not mean that a divine presence speaks, that any given language is translatable. Rather, in his view there are "laws governing translation" that lie within the original, and "translation . . . ultimately serves the purpose of expressing the innermost relationship of languages to one another."[22] Translation is, of course, the dilemma after Babel, but Benjamin's idea of translation continues the dream of Babel. It links the task of translation to that of furthering an understanding where there was once impasse or even conflict. In this way, we can note that the emphatically non-juridical law or laws that govern translation are resonant with that extra-juridical domain of nonviolence: the pre- or extra-contractual technique of ongoing conflict resolution.

For Benjamin, translation consists of a reciprocal activity of one language upon another, transforming the target language in the course of the exchange. This reciprocal activity of translation alters, intensifies, and augments each

21 Benjamin, "On Language as Such," in *Walter Benjamin: Selected Writings, Volume 1*, 69.
22 Benjamin, "Task of the Translator," 255.

language brought into contact with another, expanding the domain of communicability itself by partially realizing that non-sensible "intention" that runs through all languages. That intention can never be realized; it, too, is ongoing. This ideal of an expanding and intensifying communicability maintains an important resemblance to his reference, in "Critique of Violence," to language (*die Sprache*) as the "sphere of agreement wholly inaccessible to violence."[23] On the one hand, this technique of civil governance, described as an ongoing mode of conflict resolution, relies on language as such—that which has within it the constitutive possibility of translatability, not only between languages, but between conflicting positions within a language. Each language has within it an opening to a foreign language, an openness to being contacted and transformed by the foreign.

This emphasis on language and translation is a moment of great idealism; perhaps it is a linguistic idealism, or perhaps it is an ambiguous use of the religious figure of a divine word—a word, by the way, that is described as "divine" without any indication of a God in the background. If there is something divine, the term seems to function adjectivally. What's the relation between that divine word that unfolds through the complex process of translation and what is called "divine violence" in "Critique of Violence"? Can we relate divine violence to the scenario in which Benjamin reflects upon a civil technique of conflict resolution? That latter is explicitly called "nonviolent." Is divine violence arguably renamed as nonviolence in those passages in "A Critique of Violence" where language figures as a nonviolent domain?

---

23   Benjamin, "Critique of Violence," 245.

My suggestion that divine violence could very well be related to this technique of "nonviolent" civil governance is not a popular one, since the sudden breakage at the end of the essay portends a violence of another order. And yet, what may prove key to the reading of this essay emerges nearly parenthetically at its center: this enhanced, potentially infinite modality of understanding that Benjamin elaborates as "conflict resolution" in "Critique of Violence" may well be the resurgence of a potential in language that he began to elaborate in his earlier reflections on language and translation. If such techniques of nonviolence suspend the legal frameworks that govern our understanding of violence, then perhaps that "suspension" of legal violence is precisely what is meant by "divine violence." It is a violence done to the violence of the law, exposing its lethal operation and establishing within civil society an alternative, ongoing technique that has no need of the law.

By using "violence" in multiple ways, and in naming as violent a nonviolent technique, Benjamin points to the power of this technique to negate or suspend the totalizing framework of law. He also shows the possibility of coining "violence" in new ways, implying that the term is used to name activities that contest the legal monopoly on violence. When the "strike" is offered as a potentially revolutionary power, it is allied with this "divine violence" precisely because the strike, in its general form, refuses the binding character of a legal regime. Divine violence may well be "destructive" only because it destroys those bonds, saturated in guilt, that secure the allegiance of good citizens, good legal subjects, to violent legal regimes. In destroying legal violence, divine violence (now thought through both nonviolent conflict resolution and through translation) establishes the possibility of extra-legal exchange that attends to violence, but is itself nonviolent. From one point of view, that extra-legal exchange is called "nonviolent," whereas from the perspective of the legal regime, it is violent.

Benjamin's view was taken up by legal scholar Robert Cover, who was primarily concerned with the act of legal interpretation as carrying its own violence. He argued that "the relationship between legal interpretation and the infliction of pain remains operative even in the most routine of legal acts."[24] This is perhaps most clear in the act of sentencing, a speech act with the power to imprison someone for life, or even to take his or her life away. For as the judge interprets the law—and sentencing is the pronunciation of the interpretation that the judge arrives at—the judge acts to initiate and give justification for a punishment that then involves the police and prison guards, who restrain, hurt, render helpless, kill, or fatally abandon the prisoner. So, the speech act is not separate from those other acts. It is the initial moment of that violent process, and thus very much a violent act. After claiming that "legal interpretation is a form of bonded interpretation," Cover makes a controversial claim: "If people disappear, if they die suddenly and without ceremony in prison, quite apart from any articulated justification and authorization for their demise, then we do not have constitutional interpretation at the heart of this deed, nor do we have the deed, the death, at the heart of the

---

24   Robert M. Cover, "Violence and the Word," Yale Law School Faculty Scholarship Series, paper 2708, 1986, digitalcommons.law.yale .edu, 1607.

Constitution."[25] But what if the death in prison could have been prohibited, and the law failed to take the necessary steps? Is there not a constitutional protection for those who are at risk of dying in prison to receive the assistance and resources they need to stay alive? In other words, if prison deals death not only through the death penalty, but also through more or less systematic forms of neglecting some lives rather than others, it seems clear that a few obligatory legal protections have not been honored, even those that may well engage constitutional rights. Of course, prison deals death (slowly and quickly), but also manages life, and so maintains bodies in ways that devalue their lives. In this sense, again, the loss of grievability characterizes the living, and it surely constitutes some part of unjust and unequal treatment. We might object: surely there are basic legal entitlements to life, legal safeguards against being left to die in prison, or on the border, or at sea—legal entitlements for people to receive the assistance and resources they need to stay alive?

Cover insisted that judges are engaging in violence in their interpretive acts, including their speech acts; in his view, however much they understand themselves as conducting business at a distance from the grimmer realities of prison, they are part of the same violent system. He concluded that this violence is to be accepted and organized in ways that are justified. He proposed that "to do that violence safely and effectively, responsibility for the violence must be shared," and that "many actors" must be brought into this concerted action. Fundamentally, then, he distinguished between just

---

25   Ibid., 1624.

and unjust violent legal regimes. Violence, from this perspective, should not be random, and it should not be generated by only one actor.

Cover was interested in how we think about the conduct of judges, but his views extend to how we think about violence as suffusing the legal system. We do not leave a lawless world of violence to enter into a legal world that operates without violence. Legal violence is there, not only in sentencing practices, linked as they are with the practices of punishment and incarceration, but also in the binding character of the law. The law enjoins and proscribes us, and in doing so, it already sets in motion the threat of legal violence: if we fail to follow the law, the law will seize hold of us. Cover does not allow for an easy distinction between coercion and violence, the former posited as justified, the latter as unjustifiable. On the contrary, in his view, there are only better and worse forms of legal violence.

Cover's view is honest about the violence operating within the law and accepts that we cannot do without it, even though we must judge between its better and worse forms, since living within the terms of the law is for him obligatory. For Benjamin, the problem runs deeper. There is no way to name something as either violence or nonviolence without at once invoking the framework in which that designation makes sense. That may seem like a form of relativism—what you call violence, I do not call violence, and so on—but it is something quite different. In Benjamin's view, legal violence regularly renames its own violent character as justifiable coercion or legitimate force, thereby sanitizing the violence at stake.

Benjamin documents what happens to terms such as "violence" and "nonviolence" once we understand that the frameworks within which these definitions are secured are oscillating. He remarks that a legal regime that seeks to monopolize violence must call every threat or challenge to that regime a "violent" one. Hence, it can rename its own violence as necessary or obligatory force, even as justifiable coercion, and because it works through the law, as the law, it is legal and hence justified.

At this point, we can see how something called "critique," in Benjamin's view, which queries the production and self-validation of schemes of justification, can easily be called "violence" from the point of view of a power that seeks to suppress critique of those very schemes. Indeed, for Benjamin, any inquiry, any statement, any action that calls into question the framework of legal violence within which the justificatory scheme is established will itself be called "violent," and the opposition to such a fundamental form of querying will be understood as a legal effort to contain and quash a threat to the rule of law. On the one hand, Benjamin thus offers us a way to debunk the spurious charge that a critical relation to a legal regime is by definition a violent one, even when it pursues nonviolent means. On the other hand, the position of critique is one that does not accept the justificatory schemes established within a legal framework, that seems to have as its main aim the de-constitution of a legal regime.

We may not have to uncover the workings of divine violence to understand the dynamic of reversal that characterizes the revolutionary break with legal violence. Étienne Balibar has given us an excellent framework, in *Violence and Civility*, for understanding the duality of violence we have been tracking.[26] What we have called an "oscillation" of frameworks is described by Balibar as a perpetual process of converting violence into violence. Balibar does not espouse a politics of nonviolence, but rather one of *anti-violence*. His contention is that what Hobbes described as the violent condition of the state of nature is a form of social violence that takes place among "men." For Hobbes, the equality among men in the state of nature is nevertheless afflicted by violence, becoming a war of all against all. The invocation of sovereignty is meant to put an end to those bellicose relations, but it does so only by positing the nation as a new form of community. The nation-state exercises its sovereign violence against the "primitive" violence of the pre-national community (posited as the community of men in the state of nature). So, one violence is checked by another violence, and there seems to be no way out of this circularity, or out of a political rhythm by which state violence suppresses another violence, one that it calls "popular" or "criminal," depending on the perspective, only to be checked at some point by popular uprisings themselves deemed legitimate or as crimes against the state, depending on the framework. Balibar writes, "We can be sure that Hobbes himself would never have consciously endorsed an ambivalent interpretation of the repression of violence by a sovereign power," since that sovereign power consists of a "rational application of natural law principles."[27] But Balibar points out that "that very theory links the coercive form of law

    26 Étienne Balibar, *Violence and Civility: On the Limits of Political Philosophy*, New York: Columbia University Press, 2016.
    27 Ibid., 31.

and the state to the fact that 'natural' (and, in that sense, unlimited) violence lurks behind every contradiction that might emerge in civil society."[28] Balibar later remarks that for Hegel "the state tends to bring about the *conversion* of violence and attains its internal goal by effecting this conversion in history."[29] He further finds that: "*Gewalt*, by means of the conversion it effects, transforms itself into another *Gewalt*; violence becomes power and authority."[30] Hannah Arendt, for whom power and violence are firmly distinguished, would surely object to this formulation, but it remains unclear whether she would have a sufficient rejoinder to the problem of legal violence, whether in its Benjaminian or Hobbesian form.[31]

One tentative conclusion that follows from Balibar's analysis is that violence always appears twice, although it is unclear in each case whether "violence" or "force" would be the right translation for *Gewalt*. That conversion, or what I have been calling an "oscillation," belongs to the internal logic of violence when it is exercised by power and authority as it seeks to contain or expel "natural" or extra-juridical violence. For this reason, the naming and use of violence, and the reversals it undergoes, are all important to track, for their form is dynamic, if not dialectical: one form converts into another, and the name shifts and inverts in the course of that conversion. As a result, we cannot simply start with a definition of violence and then proceed to debate under

28 Ibid., 32.
29 Ibid., 33.
30 Ibid., 34.
31 Hannah Arendt, "On Violence," in *Crises of the Republic*, San Diego: Harcourt, 1972.

what conditions violence is justified or not, for we have first to settle the question of which framework is naming violence, through what erasures, and for what purpose. The task thus becomes to track the patterned ways that violence seeks to name as violent that which resists it, and how the violent character of a legal regime is exposed as it forcibly quells dissent, punishes workers who refuse the exploitative terms of contracts, sequesters minorities, imprisons its critics, and expels its potential rivals.

Although I do not fully follow Benjamin to his anarchist conclusion, I do agree with his contention that we cannot simply assume a definition of violence and then begin our moral debates about justification without first critically examining how violence has been circumscribed, and which version is presumed in the debate in question. A critical procedure would ask as well about the very justificatory scheme at work in such a debate, its historical origins, its presuppositions and foreclosures. The reason we cannot start by stating what kind of violence is justified and what is not is that "violence" is from the start defined within certain frameworks and comes to us always already interpreted, "worked over" by its frame. We can hardly be for or against something whose very definition eludes us, or that appears in contradictory ways for which we have no account. The historicity of that working over is congealed in the discursive framework within which "violence" appears, and that tends to be one in which legal violence—and we might add, institutional forms of violence—are generally occluded. If one refuses to answer the question of which sorts of violence are justified and which are not, because one wants to call attention to the limited justificatory schemes that frame the question, then one risks unintelligibility. And/or one comes to seem dangerous, even a kind of threat. So, on the one hand, radical critical inquiry into the legitimating grounds for a legal order can be called a "violent act"; that accusation, however, works to suppress critical thought and ultimately serves the purposes of legitimating existing law.

Is "violence" here the name given to those efforts to undermine and destroy prevailing institutions of legal violence? If so, it serves not so much to describe a set of actions as to enforce a valuation upon them, at which point it does not much matter whether or not "violence" functions as a good description for whatever inquiry, action, or inaction is at issue. In fact, the evaluation precedes and conditions the description (which does not mean that there is no referent, but only that the referential function depends upon the framework in which it becomes knowable). Whatever is called "violence" becomes regarded as violent from a particular perspective embedded in a defining framework, but those frameworks are also defined in relation to one another and can be analyzed in relation to strategies of suppression and opposition. The violence at issue is not only physical, though it often is. Even physical violence belongs to broader structures of racial, gender, and sexual violence, and if we focus on the physical blow at the expense of the broader structure, we run the risk of failing to account for those kinds of violence that are linguistic, emotional, institutional, and economic—those that undermine and expose life to harm or death, but do not take the literal form of a blow. At the same time, if we immediately abstract from the physical blow, we fail to understand the embodied character of the threat, the harm, the injury. Structural forms of violence take their toll on the body, wearing the body down, deconstituting its corporeal existence. If irrigation systems are destroyed, or if populations are abandoned to disease, are these not rightly understood as operations of violence? What about choke holds and forcible detention? Solitary confinement? Institutional violence? Torture?[32] The figure of the physical blow cannot describe the full spectrum of violence; indeed, no one figure can. We could begin to construct typologies, as many people have, but the lines between types of violence tend to blur. In the act, types of violence do blur, which is one reason a phenomenological account of how violence works as "an attack on the structure of being" is so important to a critique of institutional and structural violence, and especially that of carceral violence.[33]

That does not mean that violence can be wished away or that it is merely a matter of subjective opinion. On the contrary: violence is precisely what is perpetually subjected to an oscillation of frameworks that pivot on questions of justification and legitimacy. We can see how this works in Talal Asad's important anthropological analysis of death dealing:[34] some forms are justified, even glorified, and others are disparaged and condemned. Depending on the

32   See John Yoo's memos explaining that torture is legal and justifiable violence. John Yoo to William J. Haynes II, "Re: Military Interrogation of Alien Unlawful Combatants Held Outside the United States," March 14, 2003, US Department of Justice Office of Legal Counsel, aclu.org/files /pdfs/safefree/yoo_army_torture_memo.pdf.

33   Lisa Guenther, *Solitary Confinement: Social Death and Its Afterlives*, Minneapolis, MN: University of Minnesota Press, 2013.

34   Talal Asad, *On Suicide Bombing*, New York: Columbia University Press, 2007.

state, state-sanctioned violence is justified; non-state-based violence is unjustified. Indeed, with the support of some versions of the state, the death dealing is said to be done in the name of justice and democracy, and in non-state-based violence, the death dealing is criminal or terrorist. The methods may be similar or different, and their destructive power may be equal in intensity or equally horrific in their consequences. And yet, the fact that life is taken away in quite brutal forms within each framework does not always lead to the insight that there is a greater proximity among forms of death dealing that we might be led to expect.

The point is not to accept a general relativism. The task, rather, is to track and expose the oscillation of frameworks within which naming practices take place. For only then does it become possible to secure our understanding of what nonviolence is, and what it entails, over and against an attribution that either (a) discharges and externalizes violence onto nonviolent action or (b) expands the scope of "violence" to include critique, dissent, and non-compliance. It should not be a struggle to secure the semantics for established nonviolent tactics of resistance to legal or economic forms of exploitation or to political forms of constraint, including the strike; the hunger strike in prison; work stoppages; nonviolent forms of occupying government or official buildings or spaces, or those whose private and public status is being contested; or boycotts of various kinds, including consumer and cultural boycotts, sanctions, but also public assemblies, petitions, and all the other ways of refusing to recognize illegitimate authority. What tends to unify such actions, or inactions, is that they all call into question the legitimacy of a set of policies or actions, or even, in the case of the general strike or an anti-colonial resistance, the legitimacy of a specific form of rule. And yet, all of them, by virtue of calling for a change in police, state formation, or rule, can be called "destructive"; because they demand a substantial alteration of the status quo, raising the question of legitimacy—the ultimate exercise of critical thought—thus becomes regarded as a violent act. When "violence" comes to name nonviolent forms of resistance to legal violence, then it becomes all the more important to situate that naming practice critically within political frameworks and their self-justificatory schemes. I see this not only as a task for contemporary critical theory, but for any self-reflective ethics and politics of nonviolence.

While I take seriously Benjamin's claim that we have to think critically about how such justificatory schemes are established before we simply use them, I also think that we are obligated to make decisions that commit us to certain frameworks. As much as we cannot decide whether or not violence is justified without knowing what counts as violent, we cannot give up on the demand to decide the difference between violence and nonviolence. In other words, the operation of critique cannot preclude commitment and judgment. Benjamin's analysis questions whether any given action should be considered violent or nonviolent. The frame within which that question is posed determines in large part the way it is settled. The justificatory schemes produced by the law tend to reproduce its own legitimacy in precisely the language through which the question is at once posed and settled.

But let us add to this point a second one, namely, that structures of inequality affect the general willingness to perceive and name violence, and to grasp and declare its unjustifiability. For a nonviolent movement can, in gaining power, become an authority that wields legal violence; and a violent authority, dissolved, can relinquish a legal framework. And from the point of view of the power supported by a law that monopolizes violence as coercion, there will always be the opportunity to name those who seek the dissolution of that legal regime as threats to the nation, rogues, violent adversaries, domestic enemies, a threat to life itself. That last accusation only holds, however, when law has made itself coextensive with life. Benjamin's view is that it never fully is.

Relationality in Life

I understand that this argument leaves many questions unanswered, including the important question of whether we are referring only to human life, to cell tissue and embryonic life, or to all species and living processes, and thus to the ecological conditions of life. The point would be to rethink the relationality of life regularly covered over by typologies that distinguish forms of life. In such a relationality, I would include concepts of interdependency, and not only those among living human creatures—for human creatures living somewhere, requiring soil and water for the continuation of life, are also living in a world where non-human creatures' claim to life clearly overlaps with the human claim, and where non-humans and humans are also sometimes quite dependent on one another for life.[35] Those overlapping

---

35   Donna Haraway, *The Companion Species Manifesto*, Chicago: Prickly

zones of life (or living) have to be thought as both relational and processual, but also, each of them, as requiring conditions for the safeguarding of life.

One reason I have argued that nonviolence has to be linked to a commitment to radical equality is precisely because violence operates as an intensification of social inequality. Those inequalities are produced differently by biopolitical forms of racism and war logics, but both of them regularly distinguish among grievable and ungrievable lives, valuable and dispensable lives. The biopolitical forms of violence do not precisely follow the logics of war, but they do absorb its phantasmatic scenes into its own mode of rationality: if Europe or the US (or Australia) let migrants enter their borders, they will suffer destruction as a result of their hospitality. The new migrant is thus figured as a force of destruction who will engulf and negate its host. This fantasy becomes the basis for justifying violent destruction against migrant populations. They embody and threaten destruction and so must be destroyed. The act based on such a logic, however, reveals that the violence at issue is the violence against migrants. According to that war logic, there is a panicked standoff: at risk of suffering violence and destruction is imagined to be the condition of the state that defends itself against migrants. And yet the violence is state violence, fueled by racism and paranoia, and directed against the migrant population. The wrong committed is clearly the infliction of violence, and yet another wrong, the reproduction of social inequality, takes place at the same time: the

---

Paradigm, 2003; and *When Species Meet*, Minneapolis, MN: University of Minnesota Press, 2007.

latter takes the form of an intensification of the difference among the value accorded to lives and their very grievability. And this is why a critique of violence must also be a radical critique of inequality. Further, an opposition to inequality entails a critical exposure of the racial phantasmagoria in which some lives are figured as pure violence or as an imminent threat of violence, whereas others are regarded as entitled to self-defense and to the preservation of their lives. This power differential and its phantasmagoric form enter the conceptual apparatus by which questions of violence and nonviolence are debated and decided in public life.

The critique of violence is not the same as a practice of nonviolence, but no such practice can proceed without such a critique. The practice of nonviolence has to confront all these phantasmagoric and political challenges, and that can become a matter of despair. Of course, Fanon is now used for many purposes, including to justify violence and to work against it. But he proves central to this argument once one considers that the body, so central to *Black Skin, White Masks*, reemerges in his essay "Concerning Violence" in a way that leads to an insight into equality. Of course, in Fanon there is the fantasy of superhuman muscularity, an imagining of the body as strong enough to overthrow the fortress of colonial power—a fantasy of hyper-masculinity that many have criticized. But there is another approach to this text, one which furnishes an insight into equality that emerges from the circumstance of bodily proximity:

> The *indigène* discovers that his life, his breath, his beating heart are the same as those of the settler. He finds out that the settler's skin is not of any more value than a native's

skin; and it must be said that this discovery shakes the world in a very necessary manner. All the new, revolutionary assurance of the *indigène* stems from it. For if, in fact, my life is worth as much as the settler's, his glance no longer shrivels me up nor freezes me, and his voice no longer turns me into stone.[36]

This is a moment in which the racial phantasm breaks up and the assertion of equality shakes the world, opening up a world-making potential.

We have sought to track in general terms the way a legal regime attributes violence to those who seek to expose and bring down its structural racism. It is surely shocking when the demand for equality is called a "violent" act, or when the same condemnation is made of the demand for political self-determination or the demand to live free of securitarian threats and censorship.

How is such an attribution and projection to be articulated, criticized, and defeated? For those purposes, let us consider the conceptual inversions animated by fantasy that support the augmentation of state violence. In Turkey, those who have signed a petition for peace are accused of terrorism. And in Palestine, those who seek a political form of rule that guarantees equality and political self-determination for all are often accused of violent destructiveness. Such allegations are meant to paralyze and undermine those who advocate nonviolence, distorting the position against war as if it were all along only a position *within* a war.

---

36 Frantz Fanon, "Concerning Violence," in *The Wretched of the Earth*, trans. Constance Farrington, New York: Grove Press, 1963, 44.

When that happens, and it does, the critique of war is construed as subterfuge, aggression, dissimulated hostility. Critique, dissent, and civil disobedience are construed as attacks on the nation, the state, humanity itself. This accusation emerges from within the framework of presumptive war, where no position can be imagined outside that frame. In other words, all positions, however manifestly nonviolent, are considered to be permutations of violence. So, though I refer to practices that are "manifestly" nonviolent, it is clear that only certain practices can manifest themselves as nonviolent within an episteme governed by a paranoid and inverted logic. When the critique of war itself or the call to end social and economic inequality are considered as ways of waging war, it is easy to fall into despair and to conclude that all words can be twisted and all meanings defeated. I don't believe that that is the conclusion.

Critical patience is required, in the face of impending nihilism, to expose the forms of phantasmagoria according to which someone is "attacking" when they are not, or when that same person is, indeed, being attacked. This inversion is enacted by the view, the policy, that considers that the migration of people from the Middle East or North Africa will destroy Europe and humanity and so should be refused and abandoned, even left to die, if necessary. This murderous logic reigns among reactionaries and fascists during this time. A phantasm has substituted for whoever is speaking and acting at that moment, for whoever seems to be speaking or acting, a phantasm that embodies the aggression of those who fear the potential violence of others, and who invest and encounter destructiveness in those externalized figures—this is the lethal accomplishment of fully externalize destructiveness.

That form of defensive aggression is quite far from the insight that this life is not finally separable from another, no matter what walls are built between them. Even walls tend to bind together those they separate, usually in a wretched form of the social bond.

With this last perspective in mind, we might reapproach equality and cohabitation on new terms, starting from the presumption that all lives are equally grievable and trying to see how that matters both in death and in life, for in life the potentially grievable life is one that deserves a future, a future whose form cannot be predicted and prescribed in advance. To safeguard the future of a life is not to impose the form that such a life will take, the path that such a life will follow: it is a way of holding open the contingent and unpredictable forms that lives may take. To regard that safeguarding as an affirmative obligation proves to be quite different from preserving oneself, or one's community, at the expense of others whose difference is constantly figured as a threat. When migrants, for example, are figured as boding destruction, as pure vessels of destruction, poisoning racial or national identity with impurities, then actions that stop and detain them indefinitely, push them back into the sea, refuse to respond to their SOS when their crafts are falling apart and death is imminent, are all angrily and vindictively justified as the "self-defense" of the autochthonous community, tacitly or manifestly defined by racial privilege. In this form of morally licensed destructiveness, it turns out that destruction is emanating from a toxic and inflated notion of self-defense whose practices of renaming effect the justification of its own violence. That violence is then transferred, cloaked, and licensed by that racist moralization, one that operates in the defense of race and racism alike.

Perhaps we are describing psychic mechanisms that populate the human world, and our opposition to violence is a vain effort to change the destructive potential to be found in the human psyche or in its defining relationships. The rejoinder to a political critique of violence sometimes take the form of an argument that human destructiveness can never be fully overcome, that it belongs to human communities as a drive, pulsation, or potential that fortifies and breaks apart social bonds as we know them. Hobbes certainly had that view, and Balibar has offered a contemporary reconsideration that is most incisive. The question of whether destructiveness is a drive, or a feature, in social relations remains an open one. And even if we conceded the general possibility, or tendency, toward destructiveness, does that undermine or strengthen the political critique of violence? To address both of these questions, we would have to ask: What does destructiveness imply for social theory and political philosophy? Is it a by-product of interdependency, or part of the polarity of love and hate that characterizes human relations, part of what threatens human communities or lets them cohere?

The reconsideration of social bonds as based in embodied forms of interdependency gives us a framework for understanding a version of social equality that does not rely on the reproduction of individualism. The individual is not displaced by the collective, but is formed and freighted by social bonds that are defined by their necessity and their ambivalence. To refer to the equal grievability of lives in this context is not to establish a metric of grievability that would be applied to individuals, but to ask after the racial phantasms that inform public ideas about what kind of life deserves an open-ended future, and whose lives are grievable.

The dismantling of that phantasmatic domain in which lives are differentially valued requires an affirmation of life, one that is different from a "pro-life" position. Indeed, the left should not sacrifice the discourse on life to its reactionary opponents. To affirm equality is to affirm a cohabitation defined in part by an interdependency that takes the edge off the individual boundaries of the body, or that works that edge for its social and political potential.

Such an affirmation of life is not just of my life, although my life would surely be included: it would prove to be quite different from a self-preservation won at the expense of other lives, fortified by figures of aggression that project the destructive potential of every social bond in ways that break the social bond itself. Even if none of us are freed of the capacity for destruction, or precisely because none of us are freed of that capacity, that ethical and political reflection converges on the task of nonviolence. It is precisely because we can destroy that we are under an obligation to know why we ought not to do it, and to summon those countervailing powers that curb our destructive capacity. Nonviolence becomes an ethical obligation by which we are bound precisely because we are bound to one another; it may well be an obligation against which we rail, in which ambivalent swings of the psyche make themselves known, but the obligation to preserve the social bond can be resolved upon without precisely resolving that ambivalence. The obligation not to destroy each other emerges from, and reflects, the vexed social form of our lives, and it leads us to reconsider whether self-preservation is not linked to preserving the lives of others. The self of self-preservation is defined, in part, by that link, that necessary and difficult social bond.

If self-preservation were to become the ground for waging violence, if it were to become enshrined as the exception to principles of nonviolence, then who would that "self" be who preserves itself and only those who belong already to the regime of itself? Such a self belongs only to itself or to those who augment its sense of itself, and so stands world-less, threatening this world.

4

Political Philosophy in Freud:
War, Destruction, Mania,
and the Critical Faculty

I fear I may be abusing your interest, which is after all
concerned with the prevention of war and not with
our theories. Nevertheless, I should like to linger for a
moment over our destructive drive, whose popularity is
by no means equal to its importance.

Sigmund Freud to Albert Einstein, 1932

In his "Thoughts for the Times on War and Death," written
in 1915 and in the midst of the First World War, Sigmund
Freud reflected on the bonds that hold a community
together, as well as the destructive powers that break those
bonds.[1] By the time he developed the "death drive," first in

---

1   Sigmund Freud, "Thoughts for the Times on War and Death," in
The Standard Edition of the Complete Psychological Works of Sigmund Freud,
trans. James Strachey, vol. 14, London: Hogarth Press, 1915, 273–300.

1920² and then more fully in the following decade, he had become increasingly concerned with the destructive capacities of human beings. What he calls "sadism," "aggression," and "destructiveness" came to be primary representatives of the death drive, which received its most mature formulation in *Civilization and Its Discontents* in 1930.³ What he had called an "unconquerable part of human nature" in *Beyond the Pleasure Principle* ten years earlier here takes on a new form as Freud develops a dualistic metaphysics, counterposing Eros, the force that creates ever more complex human bonds, to Thanatos, the force that breaks them down. A durable political form presumes that social bonds can remain relatively in place; but how, then, do polities deal with the destructive force that Freud describes?

Freud's reflections on World War I led to successive insights on destructiveness. In 1915, Freud had not yet introduced the notion of the death drive—of which one of the primary aims would be the deterioration of social bonds—but he did register an impression of overwhelming and unprecedented human destructiveness in his time:

> The war in which we had refused to believe broke out and brought—disillusionment. Not only is it more bloody and more destructive than any war of other days, because of the enormously increased perfection of weapons of attack and defence; it is at least as cruel, as embittered, as implacable as any that has preceded it. It disregards all the restrictions

Abbreviated "SE" in subsequent citations.
2   Sigmund Freud, *Beyond the Pleasure Principle*, SE vol. 18, 1920.
3   Sigmund Freud, *Civilization and Its Discontents*, SE vol. 21, 1930.

known as International Law, which in peace-time the states had bound themselves to observe; it ignores the prerogatives of the wounded and the medical service, the distinction between civil and military sections of the population, the claims of private property. It tramples in blind fury on all that comes in its way, as though there were to be no future and no peace among men after it is over. It cuts all the common bonds between the contending peoples, and threatens to leave a legacy of embitterment that will make any renewal of those bonds impossible for a long time to come.[4]

Freud's remarks are noteworthy for many reasons, chief among them the sense of a shift in the history of destructiveness: destructiveness has not been known quite like this before. Although the development of new weapons has made the destruction greater than in previous wars, the level of cruelty strikes Freud as the same, suggesting that the problem is not that humans have become more cruel, but that technology has allowed that cruelty to produce greater destruction than before. A war without those weapons would cause less destruction but would engage no lesser amount of cruelty. So, if we are tempted to say that cruelty is itself augmented by technology, Freud appears to resist that view: destruction takes on new and historically variable forms, but cruelty remains the same. Thus, human cruelty alone does not account for all destructiveness—technology exercises its agency as well. But the distinctly human capacity for destructiveness in human beings follows from

---

4   Freud, "War and Death," 278–9.

the ambivalent psychic constitution of the human subject. The question of what can be done to check destructiveness thus engages ambivalence and technology, especially in the context of war.

Although it is commonly supposed that war making is the specific activity of nations, the blind rage that motivates war destroys the very social bonds that make nations possible. Of course, it can fortify the nationalism of a nation, producing a provisional coherence bolstered by war and enmity, but it also erodes the social relations that make politics possible. The power of destruction unleashed by war breaks social ties and produces anger, revenge, and distrust ("embitterment") such that it becomes unclear whether reparation is possible, undermining not only those relations that may have been built in the past, but also the future possibility of peaceful coexistence. Although Freud is clearly reflecting on World War I in his remarks above, he is also making claims about war in general: war "tramples . . . on all that comes in its way." Here, he is suggesting that breaking down the barriers that keep inhibitions in place is, in fact, one aim of war—military personnel have to be given license to kill. Whatever the explicit strategic or political aims of a war may be, they prove to be weak in comparison with its aims of destruction; what war destroys first are the very restrictions imposed on destructive license. If we can rightly speak about the unstated "aim" of war, it is neither primarily to alter the political landscape nor to establish a new political order, but rather to destroy the social basis of politics itself. Of course, such a claim may seem overstated if we believe, for instance, in just wars—wars waged against fascist or genocidal regimes in the name of democracy. But even then, the explicit goal of war waging and the destructiveness unleashed by war are never quite the same. Even so-called "just war" runs the risk of a destructiveness that exceeds its stated aims, its deliberate purpose.

Indeed, whatever the public and stated aims of war may be, another aim is always also at work, one that Freud refers to here as "blind fury." Moreover, this fury, motivating and even unifying a people or a nation at war, also tears the people and the nation apart, working against whatever intentional, self-preserving, or self-enhancing aims they may have. This sort of rage aims, first and foremost, to overcome existing inhibitions and restrictions imposed on destruction itself, to break social bonds—understood in part as blocks against destruction—in favor of increased destructiveness, and to reproduce destruction into the foreseeable future, which may turn out to be either a future of destruction or a way of destroying the future itself. It is from within the stated local and provisional aims for war making that another aim, or indeed a "drive," can take hold—a destructiveness without limit. Even as a group or a nation may achieve temporary cohesion in war, rallying behind its explicit aims to defend the country or to destroy the enemy, something can form— or take hold—within that rallying that exceeds any of those explicitly acknowledged aims, breaking not only the social bonds of the groups targeted by war but those of the groups waging war, as well. The idea of "blind fury" that Freud takes from Greek tragedy prefigures what he would come to call the "death drive" just five years later. Already in 1915, what concerns him is the power that the death drive assumes, once it is amplified with destructive technology, to wreak destruction across the world, and to destroy the very social bonds that have the power to keep destructiveness in check. By 1930, Freud would become more explicitly concerned with the possibility of genocide, as evidenced in *Civilization and Its Discontents*. There, he writes:

> The fateful question for the human species seems to me to be whether and to what extent their cultural development will succeed in mastering the disturbance of their communal life by the human instinct [*Trieb*] of aggression and self-destruction [*Agressions und Selbstvernichtungstrieb*]. It may be that in this respect precisely the present time deserves a special interest. Men have gained control over the forces of nature to such an extent that with their help they would have no difficulty in exterminating one another to the last man.[5]

In the 1931 edition, he appended a line to that paragraph calling upon "eternal Eros . . . to assert himself in the struggle with his equally immortal adversary," noting that no one can foresee how successful that effort will be. Freud was clearly looking for a possibility to counter the horrific destructiveness that he saw in the First World War and that he sensed was returning to Europe in greater proportions in the 1930s. Freud does not turn to history or to empirical examples in his effort to understand destructiveness, but to what he calls the "drives"—a move that seems speculative at best. So why look to the life of the drives? For Freud, the conscious reasons for acting that groups give to themselves are not the same as the underlying motivations that guide their action.

---

5   Freud, *Civilization and Its Discontents*, 145.

As a result, reflection on how best to avert destruction must do something other than provide an argument acceptable to rational thought—it must somehow appeal to the drive, or find a way of working with—and against—that propulsive destructiveness that can lead to war.

One skeptical position toward drive theory results from a mistaken translation of Freud's "*Trieb*" as "instinct." Although *Instinkt* and *Trieb* are both used in Freud's work, the latter appears more often, and the death drive (*Todestrieb*) is never "the death instinct." The James Strachey translation of the *Complete Works* consistently renders both terms as "instinct," giving rise to a biologistic understanding of the term in English-language literature and, in some cases, a view that drives, in Freud, follow a form of biological determinism. Freud makes clear, in an essay entitled "Instincts and Their Vicissitudes" ("*Triebe und Triebschicksale*," better translated as "Drives and Their Destinies"), that the drive (*Trieb*, meaning "push") belongs neither exclusively to the realm of biology nor to a fully autonomous psychic domain; rather, it functions as a threshold concept (*ein Grenzbegriff*) between somatic and ideational spheres.[6]

Until 1920, Freud maintained that psychic life was governed by pleasure, sexuality, or libido, and it was only when he encountered forms of war neurosis that he began to consider that there were symptoms characterized by compulsive repetition that could not be explained by wish fulfillment or a drive toward

---

6 Freud, "Instincts and Their Vicissitudes," SE vol. 14, 1915, 121–22: "An 'instinct' appears to us as a concept on the frontier between the mental and the somatic." In German: "So erscheint uns der 'Trieb' als ein Grenzbegriff zwischen Seelischem und Somatischem." Sigmund Freud, *Psychologie des Unbewussten*, Frankfurt am Main: Fischer Verlag, 1982, 85.

gratification. So, it was in the wake of war that Freud began to formulate the death drive, prompted as well by his consideration of forms of destructiveness, particularly those with a repetitive quality (what he would later refer to as "non-erotic aggressivity" in *Civilization and Its Discontents*).[7] It was in the first formulation of the death drive, in *Beyond the Pleasure Principle*, that Freud sought to find an explanation for forms of repetitive behavior that did not appear to serve any wishes. He had encountered patients suffering from war neurosis who relived traumatic scenes of violence and loss in ways that bore no clear resemblance to forms of repetition accounted for by the pleasure principle. Not only was there no apparent satisfaction linked to this repetitious suffering, it progressively deteriorated the condition of the patient to the point of imperiling the organic basis of the patient's life. At this stage, Freud developed the first version of the death drive, according to which the organism seeks a return to its primary inorganic state, a state relieved of all excitation. Indeed, every human organism seeks to return to this origin, such that the trajectory of a life turns out to be no more than a "circuitous route toward death."[8] As much as there is something in humans that seeks to fulfill wishes and to preserve its own organic life, there is also something that operates to the side of wish fulfillment, seeking to negate the organic conditions of life, whether that life belongs to another, to oneself, or to the living environment in its dynamic complexity.

What difference does it make that Freud now posits another tendency within the human psyche that seeks

---

7   Freud, *Civilization and Its Discontents*, 120.
8   Freud, *Beyond the Pleasure Principle*, 38.

to return it to a time before the individuated life of the human organism? His reflections on destruction focus on the possibility of the destruction of other lives, especially under conditions of war, in which the technology of weaponry amplifies the powers of human destructiveness. Those who suffered war neurosis were living out the psychic consequences of war, but they also became the occasion for Freud to consider how destruction works not only against others, but against oneself. War neurosis continues the suffering of war in the form of traumatic symptoms characterized by relentless repetition; one is bombarded, attacked, under siege—all metaphors of war that continue in the posttraumatic scene. Freud identifies this as the repetitive character of destruction. In the patient, it eventuates in social isolation; more broadly considered, it not only serves to weaken the social bonds that hold societies together, but also takes form as a self-destruction that can culminate in suicide. Libido or sexuality has a reduced or vanishing role in this form of destruction, and the social bonds without which political life proves impossible are shredded in its midst.

Toward the end of *Beyond the Pleasure Principle*, Freud asserts not only that every human organism in some sense seeks its own death, but that this tendency cannot be derived from the sexual drives. The evidence for the death drive, he argues, can be found within sexual sadism and, more generally, within the phenomenon of sadomasochism.[9] Although

---

9 Freud's theorization of sadomasochism seeks first to explain the phenomenon through recourse to the theory of libido in "Instincts and Their Vicissitudes" (1915), but it is revised in light of the death drive in

the sexualization of the death drive can subordinate its destructiveness to what Freud regards as the non-destructive aims of sexuality, the death drive can come to predominate— a situation illustrated clearly with sexual violence. Both self-destruction and the destruction of the other are potentially at work within sadomasochism, suggesting for Freud that a drive separate from the sexual drive can nevertheless operate through it. Fugitive and opportunistic, the death drive seizes upon sexual desire without properly or explicitly making itself known. A sexual relation that begins with the desire to join together becomes interrupted by myriad forms of self-destruction that seem manifestly counter to the stated aims of the lovers. The disconcerting quality of acts that are clearly self-destructive, or that destroy the bonds that one wants most to keep, is but one ordinary form of wreckage by which the death drive makes itself known in sexual life.

In *Civilization and Its Discontents*, Freud once again introduces sadism as the "representative" of the death drive, but in this late work he links the death drive more explicitly with the concepts of aggression and destructiveness. This can be understood as the second, or later, version of the death drive. Aggression is no longer understood as operating exclusively in the context of sexual sadomasochism, for, as Freud remarks, "we can no longer overlook the ubiquity of non-erotic aggressivity and destructiveness."[10] Freud is registering the escalation of bellicosity and nationalism across Europe, as well as the strengthening of anti-Semitism. These

---

Beyond the Pleasure Principle (1920) and then in "The Economic Problem of Masochism" (SE vol. 19, 1924).

10   Freud, *Civilization and Its Discontents*, 120.

forms of aggression are not linked with pleasure or with the satisfactions that belong to pleasure: "This aggressive instinct [drive] is the derivative and the main representative of the death instinct [drive] which we have found alongside of Eros and which shares world-dominion with it."[11] Even though what he now calls "Eros" and "Thanatos" do not usually occur separately, they nevertheless have contrary aims: Eros seeks to combine or synthesize separate units within society, bringing individuals together into groups, but also bringing groups together in the service of larger social and political forms. Thanatos drives those same units apart from one another as well as each unit apart from itself. So, in the very action that seeks to establish and build a social bond, a counter-tendency exists that just as readily seeks to take it apart: I love you, I hate you; I cannot live without you, I will die if I continue to live with you.

Freud has two different ways of approaching this problem in relation to love. On the one hand, Freud insists throughout his work on the constitutive ambivalence of all love relations. This becomes clear in his chapter on "emotional ambivalence" in *Totem and Taboo*,[12] but also in "Mourning and Melancholia," where the loss of the loved one is coupled with aggression.[13] On that model, love is itself ambivalent.[14] On the other hand, "love," another name for "Eros," names only one pole in the polarity of emotional ambivalence. There is love and there is hate. So, either love

---

11   Ibid., 122.
12   Freud, *Totem and Taboo*, SE vol. 14, 1913.
13   Freud, "Mourning and Melancholia," SE vol. 14, 1917, 248–52.
14   Ibid., 250.

names the ambivalent constellation of love and hate, or it is but one pole of that bipolar structure. Freud's own position seems itself to be ambivalent, perhaps rhetorically yielding further proof of his claim. Indeed, the paradoxical formulation is never fully resolved in his writings, remaining fecund throughout. It surfaces symptomatically in the late work: love is that which binds one person to another, but love, by virtue of its inherent ambivalence, contains the potential to destroy social bonds. Or, at least, if it is not love that destroys those bonds, there is a destructive force that is in love or attaches itself to love—one that moves human creatures toward destruction and self-destruction, including the destruction of that which they most love.

The fact that Freud's view remains unsettled on the question of whether love contains or opposes this destructiveness is a sign of a problem that continues as he attempts to think about not only intimate relations of love, but the psychology of the mass and its destructive potential. Is the destructive capacity to be found within the bonds that hold such groups together—a sort of destructive tie—or is it rather a power that "cuts all the common bonds"—an anti-social impetus that tears at social relations?

What within the psyche militates against this cutting of social bonds? In Freud's view, groups can either destroy their internal bonds, or they can direct their destructiveness toward other groups; both forms of destructiveness, he worries, are assisted by an inhibition of the critical faculty. So, the task that emerges for Freud, in his writings on group psychology, is to strengthen the inhibiting power of this critical faculty. Whereas love is sometimes identified as the counter-force to destruction, at other times it seems it is this "critical faculty" that is most important. In his 1921 monograph *Group Psychology and the Analysis of the Ego*, the "critical faculty" describes various forms of deliberation and reflection; however, the next year, in *The Ego and the Id*, the critical faculty becomes associated with the "super-ego," a form of cruelty unleashed upon the ego. Eventually, the super-ego will come to be identified as "a pure culture of the death drive," at which point the way to counter destruction is through deliberate forms of self-restraint, that is, by directing destructiveness against one's own destructive impulse. Self-restraint is thus a deliberate and reflexive form of destructiveness, directed against the externalization of destructive aims.[15] In other words, the check against unleashing destructive impulse, which in its earlier iteration could have been described as an "inhibition," is set up as a psychic mechanism bent on cruelty once Freud introduces the super-ego. The task of the super-ego is to direct its destructive power against its destructive impulses. The problem with this solution, of course, is that an unbridled operation of the super-ego can lead to suicide, converting the destruction of the other into the destruction of the self. On the one hand, the "critical faculty" seems attentive to the consequences of action, monitoring forms of expression and action to prevent injurious consequences. On the other hand, as an expression of the death drive, its aim is potentially destructive of the ego itself. A moderate form of self-checking can explode into unrestrained suicidal self-beratement, but only if the death drive itself remains unchecked. Paradoxically, this means that the critical agency

---

15   Freud, *The Ego and the Id*, SE vol. 19, 1923, 53.

upon which one relies to check destructive impulse can become an internalized instrument of destructive impulse, imperiling the life of the ego itself. Thus, the self-preserving tendencies of Eros have to be applied to the death drive as a check on its destructive operation. If the super-ego works destruction against the ego in order to inhibit the latter's destructive expression, it still traffics in destruction, but the imperiled object is no longer the other or the world, but the ego itself. Thus, the critical faculty is of limited use in checking destruction, since it cannot check the destruction that operates through its super-egoic form. For that, a countervailing force is needed, one that pursues self-preservation and, more generally, the preservation of life. Is that force to be called love, or is it mania? Does it involve dis-identification, or the adoption of a neurotic position that establishes a critical distance from the sadistic exhilarations that run through society?

In *Group Psychology and the Analysis of the Ego*, written a year or so before the development of the theory of the super-ego, Freud asks: What is the mechanism by which the dis-inhibition of cruelty takes place? How do we account for its workings? When we say that a "wave of feeling" passes through a crowd, what do we mean? Or, when certain kinds of passions that would otherwise remain unexpressed are "unleashed" in a crowd, how do we account for that expression? Does "unleashing" mean that a desire was always there, but that it was simply held in check? Or is "unleashing" always structured, thus giving form to the desire or rage as it emerges? If we say that an elected official has licensed a new wave of misogyny, or that he has made widespread racism permissible, what sort of agency do we attribute to him?

Was it there all along, or has he brought it into being? Or is it that it was there in certain forms, and now his speech and action give it new ones? In either case, impulse is structured either by the power by which it is "repressed" (which designates and shapes it in some way) or by that power by which it is "liberated" (which endows it with specific meaning in relation to the prior repression). If we were simply to accept a hydraulic model—one that holds that a quantity of "energy" is released when inhibition is lifted—then the impulse is the same whether it is inhibited or expressed. But if it matters through what means the inhibition has been enforced, and if that means crafts the content of the repressed, then the emergence of the formerly inhibited impulse does not simply push aside the inhibiting force; rather, it wages an orchestrated attack on that form of power, debunking its reasons, its legitimacy, its claims. The impulse that emerges is thus worked over by interpretations, and so there is no raw or unmediated energy to be subjected to the mechanisms of prohibition or license. This impulse has actively contested the moral and political claims that have informed and supported the inhibition; it has worked assiduously against the critical faculty—not just against moral judgments and political evaluations, but against the general character of reflective thought that makes both possible. The impulse seeks to disperse and nullify moral self-restriction, itself the basis for what Freud comes to call the "super-ego." It may seem that against such a challenge to the super-ego, the task is to shore up moral restrictions, especially those that the self imposes on itself. But once it becomes clear that the super-ego is itself a potential force of destruction, the matter becomes more complex.

Freud puts the matter this way:

> The excessively strong super-ego which has obtained a
> hold on consciousness rages against the ego with merciless
> violence, as if it had taken possession of the whole of the
> sadism available in the person ... What is now holding
> sway in the super-ego is, as it were, a pure culture of the
> death drive, and in fact it often enough succeeds in driv-
> ing the ego into death.[16]

What, if anything, checks the merciless violence of one part
of the self unleashed against another? Freud finishes that
sentence by claiming that one way to thwart the success of
self-destruction is for the ego to "fend off its tyrant in time
by the change round into mania."

Freud here references his 1917 work "Mourning and
Melancholia," where he seeks to distinguish between "mourning," which implies a wakeful acknowledgment of the reality
of a lost person or ideal, and "melancholia," which is a failure
to acknowledge the reality of loss. In melancholia, the lost
other is internalized (in the sense that it is incorporated) as a
feature of the ego, and a form of heightened self-beratement
reenacts—and inverts—at a psychic level the relation of the
ego to the lost other. The recrimination against the lost person
or ideal is "turned round" against the ego itself; in this way,
the relation is preserved as an animated intra-psychic relation.[17] Even in that essay, Freud makes clear that the hostility
unleashed against the ego is potentially fatal. The scene of

---

16   Ibid., translation modified.
17   Freud, "Mourning and Melancholia," 251.

melancholic self-beratement thus becomes the model for the later topography of super-ego and ego.

Melancholia is composed of two opposing trends: the first is self-beratement, which becomes the signature action of "conscience"; the second is "mania," which seeks to break the bond to the lost object, actively renouncing the object that is gone.[18] The "manic" and energetic denunciations of the object, the ego's heightened efforts to break the bond to the lost object or ideal, imply the desire to survive the loss and not to have one's own life claimed by the loss itself. Mania is, as it were, the protest of the living organism against the prospect of its destruction by an unchecked super-ego. So, if the super-ego is the continuation of the death drive, mania is the protest against destructive action directed toward the world and toward the self. Mania asks: "Is there any way out of this vicious circle in which destructiveness is countered by self-destructiveness?"

Too often, the path is traced from melancholia to the super-ego, but the countervailing tendency, mania, may hold clues to a different kind of resistance to destruction. The manic force that seeks the overthrow of the tyrant is in some ways a power of the organism to break what have been regarded as sustaining bonds of identification. The organism is already a threshold concept where the somatic and psychic meet, so this is not a purely naturalistic upsurge of rebellious life. *Dis-identification* becomes one way to counter the powers of self-destruction and to secure the living on of the organism itself. To the degree that mania breaks bonds, dis-identifies with the tyrant

---

18   Ibid., 253–5.

and the subjection that tyranny requires, it takes on a critical function—engaging and seeking to resolve a crisis, taking distance from a form of power that threatens the life of the organism. The super-ego is a psychic institution, in Freud's view, but as an institution, it also takes on a social form; thus, tyranny relies on psychic subjection at the same time that the super-ego absorbs forms of social power such as tyranny. The struggle of the critical function is to break with bonds that have secured one's own destruction without precisely replicating the social form of destructiveness from which one seeks emancipation. The criticism of the tyrant, therefore, is, or can be, an exercise of a critical faculty that is directed against the super-ego without replicating its life-threatening version of "criticism."

Mania proves to be the only hope for prevailing against the suicidal and murderous aims of the unbridled super-ego that would, unleashed, judge the ego unto death, since only with that power is it possible to break with the tyrant, and with the logic of the tyrant that has become the structure of subjectification.

I surely do not want to champion mania, but only to insist that it does offer a cipher for understanding those "unrealistic" forms of insurrectionary solidarity that turn against authoritarian and tyrannical rule. The tyrant, after all, is an anthropomorphism sustained by networks of power, and so its overthrow is manic, solidaristic, and incremental. And when the head of state is himself a tyrannical child who throws fits in all directions, and the media follows his every move with rapt attention, a great space is opened up for those who might build their networks of solidarity, who might "break free" of the fascination with his strategic ways of losing control. To the degree that those who follow the mad tyrant identify with his willful disregard for law, and for any limits imposed upon his own power and destructive capacity, the counter-movement is one that is based on dis-identification.[19] Those forms of solidarity are not based on identification with the leader, but with a dis-identification that operates under the signifier of "life" but is not for that reason reductively vitalist: its stands for another life, future life.

Identifications are generally regarded as important for empathy and the perpetuation of social bonds, but they also imply destructive potential, and they permit destructive acts to be undertaken with impunity. It is no doubt important to consider the various forms of internalization that are sometimes too quickly called "identification." The internalization of the lost other or ideal, in the case of melancholia, preserves and animates a form of hostility that has the power to destroy the living organism itself. So, even as the super-ego checks the externalization of destructiveness, it remains a potentially destructive instrument that can come to serve the very murderous purposes it is meant to check in the most self-destructive way, namely, through suicide. The moralistic conclusion of Freud in this context is that the super-ego will always be a weak instrument with which to enforce a check on violence, unless we opt for the *violence of the super-ego*, however fatal that may prove, over

---

19 See José Esteban Muñoz, *Disidentifications: Queers of Color and the Performance of Politics*, Minneapolis, MN: University of Minnesota Press, 1999.

its alternative, externalized expression. But mania, evidenced in the manic desire to live, is a cipher that presents us with another possibility. It is not a model for action—the task is not suddenly to become manic, as if that would translate directly into a form of effective political resistance. It would not. Mania overestimates the power of the subject and loses touch with reality. And yet, where do we find the psychic resources for taking leave of reality as it is currently established and naturalized? The "unrealism" of mania suggests a refusal to accept the status quo, and it draws upon, and intensifies, a desire to live on the part of one who is battling against forms of heightened self-beratement. That same self-cruelty or self-destruction can be provisionally ameliorated, as well, through falling back upon the social solidarity of failure—in which none of us lives up to the ideal, and this shared failure grounds our solidarity and sense of equality. That amelioration of super-egoic violence proves to be provisional when a group formation fails to organize and contain that hostility, and it can assume a fatal form. Moreover, there are group formations that mobilize that destructive hostility toward an external enemy, at which point the destruction of life, even the mass destruction of life, becomes possible. Identification can imply destructive potential when a group forms bonds of identification that depend upon the externalization of its own destructive potential. Those others with whom the group dis-identifies come to embody that destruction in spectral form—the one that is, as it were, on (disavowed) loan from the original group. But identification does not have to work that way. When, for instance, dis-identification indicates the emergence of a critical capacity that breaks with forms of tyranny, it works with its own

powers of destruction, understood as the purposeful dismantling of a tyrannical regime.[20] This can, and does, happen
within the solidarity of sentiments, but even that is never
a perfect mode of identification: ambivalent bonds that are
nevertheless necessary for alliances, and that are mindful of
the affirmative and destructive potentials that follow from
that vexed relation. When dis-identification interrupts the
fascinated subjection to the tyrant, then dis-identification is
at once manic and critical.

If the super-ego is prized as the only possible check on
destructiveness, then destructiveness returns to the subject,
but imperils its existence. In melancholia, hostility is not
externalized, but the ego becomes the object of potentially
murderous hostility, one that wields the power to destroy
the living ego, the organism itself. But mania introduces this
unrealistic desire to exist and persist, the one that seems based
in no perceptible reality and has no good grounds for being
so within a particular political regime. On its own, mania
can never become a politics without becoming a dangerous
form of destruction, but it introduces a vigorous "unrealism"
into the modes of solidarity that seek to dismantle violent
regimes, insisting, against the odds, on another reality.

Checking Violence

Freud and Einstein are both concerned with what checks
destructiveness: whether another drive can triumph over the
death drive, whether the check requires an intensification of

20 Ibid.

conscience. For the most part, we have been left with two alternatives. One claims that we must educate ourselves and others into forms of conscience that inculcate the moral revulsion against violence. The other holds that we must foster bonds of love in order to defeat the death drive in its mechanical persistence. But if conscience can support social bonds that are nationalist, fascist, and racist, how can we rely on conscience to check violence? Obedience to a tyrannical power often requires, and enforces, a form of the subject whose self-subjugation becomes a moral imperative. To throw off tyrannical control risks the dissolution of that subject form, especially when it has become instated in super-egoic form. If we could turn to love and simply fan its flames so that it becomes the more powerful force, we would have a solution. But love, as noted above, is defined by its ambivalence, structured by the oscillation between love and hatred. The task appears to be finding a way to live and act with ambivalence—one where ambivalence is understood not as an impasse, but as an internal partition that calls for an ethical orientation and practice. For only the ethical practice that knows its own destructive potential will have the chance to resist it. Those for whom destruction is always and only coming from the outside will never be able to acknowledge, or work with, the ethical demand imposed by nonviolence. That said, violence and nonviolence remain issues that are at once socio-political and psychic, and the ethical reflection on the debate therefore must take place precisely at the threshold of the psychic and social worlds.

That very problem emerges in the correspondence between Freud and Einstein in 1931–32, the years directly preceding Hitler's rise to power and their subsequent exiles from Austria and Germany, respectively.[21] Einstein writes to Freud to ask him how humankind can become delivered from "the menace of war."[22] Lamenting that the fate of humankind is in the hands of "a governing class" that is "craving for power" and "hostile to any limitation of national sovereignty," Einstein appeals to Freud as someone whose "critical judgment" is most important at this time in which world war once again threatens Europe. He asks whether there is a basis in the drives that constitute human psychic life for a political arrangement that could serve as an effective check on war. In particular, he asks whether it might be possible to establish an association or a tribunal that could check the destructive power of those drives. Einstein first identifies the problem as destructive drives, but he also interrogates the issue at the level of political institutions, calling for nations to cede their sovereignty to an international body that would demand a commitment to preventing war and guaranteeing international security. This political goal can only be achieved if human beings are the kinds of creatures capable of constituting, and submitting to, international authorities that have the power to prevent war. If there is a tendency or drive that undercuts that capacity, then averting war may well be impossible. Clearly having read Freud, Einstein asks whether human beings have within them "a lust for hatred

21 Einstein departed Germany in 1933 and Freud left Vienna in 1938. Their correspondence can be found as "Why War?," SE vol. 22, [1933], 195–216. In 1931, the International Institute of Intellectual Cooperation invited Einstein to engage in a dialogue with a thinker of his choice on the topics of politics and peace, and he chose Freud, whom he had met briefly a few years before.

22 Einstein to Freud, "Why War?," 199.

and destruction," and whether this can be "raise[d] . . . to the power of a collective psychosis." So, though he wonders whether the destructive drives can be contained, he also wonders whether human practices or institutions can be cultivated that would increase the possibility of preventing war. He notes that violence can take the form of wars between nations, but also that of civil wars motivated by religious zealotry, as well as that of "the persecution of racial minorities."[23]

Freud warns that he has no practical proposals, but his remarks do elaborate a political position. His first proposal is to replace a distinction Einstein makes between right and power with one between right and violence ("right" translates *Recht*, which in German means legal order and even justice). In Freud's account, conflicts between persons and groups traditionally have been resolved through recourse to violence, but this has happened less regularly as group formations have changed. He notes that "a path was traced that led away from violence to law" when "an alliance of many weaklings" overcame the strength of the single man or leader.[24] In this way, he writes, "brute force is overcome through union" or what he also calls "the power of a community." In his view, "the superior strength of a single individual could be rivaled by the union of several weak ones"; and later he elaborates: "In order that the transition from violence to this new right or justice may be effected . . . the union of the majority must be a stable and lasting one." To do this, a psychological condition has to be met: "the growth

---

23   Ibid., 201.
24   Freud to Einstein, "Why War?," 205.

of . . . communal feelings which are the true source of its strength."[25]

Writing to Einstein a full decade after *Group Psychology and the Analysis of the Ego*, Freud now conjectures that the community is held together *not* by their common subordination to an ideal leader, but precisely through their explicit power to overthrow a tyrant or authoritarian ruler, and to establish common and enforceable laws and institutions in the wake of that overthrow. In order to overthrow the tyrant, and to break with attachments based on the love of the tyrant, perhaps some form of mania is required. Can mania take form within those "communal feelings" and "emotional ties" that are required to achieve that goal? The answer seems to depend on how we interpret the "community of interests."[26] Freud's wager is that as power (not violence) is transferred to ever-larger combinations, group members are increasingly enfranchised and more inclined to act from sentiments of solidarity. Einstein talked about the obligation of each nation-state to surrender its sovereignty to a larger international body. Freud also imagines the distribution of power beyond the model of sovereignty. As the community and its powers of self-governance expand and become increasingly distinct from, even opposed to, the individual ruler, "the sentiment of solidarity," expressed in a set of laws both self-legislated and self-restraining, is relied upon to check destructiveness. The ongoing problem, however, is that violence can erupt within the community, for instance when one faction pits itself against another, or when the right of

25 Ibid.
26 Ibid.

rebellion is exercised against the state or the international body that limits the sovereignty of states.

The limitation on violence seems to coincide, for both Freud and Einstein, with the limitation of state sovereignty within a broader internationalist frame. This move takes aim at the anthropomorphism of power that constitutes sovereignty itself. In the early 1930s, both Freud and Einstein understood nationalist fervor to lead to outbreaks of violence, though neither could fully see the forms of state violence in fascism and Nazism that would materialize in the next few years. The international body or "tribunal" they both imagined was to some degree represented by the League of Nations in the early 1930s, but that institution hardly constituted an ultimate power, since state sovereignty could not be effectively checked by existing institutions. Without the power of enforcement, such a body lacks the sovereign power it requires to prevent war. The conclusion, therefore, was that the ceding of sovereignty in favor of international relations was the only path to peace. Einstein, who called himself "immune from nationalist bias," thought that the risk of an international institution was worth taking: "The quest for international security involves the unconditional surrender by every nation, in a certain measure, of its liberty of action, its sovereignty that is to say, and it is clear beyond all doubt that no other road can lead to such security." He then continues to remark upon the failure of this effort, which "leaves us no room for doubt that strong psychological factors are at work."[27] For Freud, the question was how best to understand sentiments of solidarity if and

---

27   Einstein to Freud, "Why War?," 200.

when they oppose the tyrant, that is to say, if they are not based on identification with that anthropomorphic figure of unchecked power. Of course, mania is one way of taking issue with reality—that is why it belongs to the circuit of melancholia. Mania acts as if it were an unconditioned freedom, only to return to the problem of a conditioned life. But what decides that condition? And what follows once the existing conditions for exercising freedom are called into question? Some fleeting glimpse of utopia follows— transient, of course, but not for that reason without political potential.

Freud's final effort to ascertain ways to prevent war takes him on a train of thought unpursued in his reflections on group psychology: the first course he explores requires a resistance to the exhilarations of nationalism; the second makes a call to heed the "organic" basis of our nature as human beings. Lastly, he makes a strong case that there are only two ways to counter the propensity for war: the mobilization of "Eros, its antagonist," and the forming of communal forms of identification.[28] To this end, Freud speculated that an evolution of the masses may be possible through education and the cultivation of solidaristic sentiments of a non-nationalist sort.[29] The ideal condition would be one in which every member of a community exercises self-restraint, and does so precisely by recognizing that the preservation of life is itself a good to be valued in common. Freud's ideal of a community, one whose members are equally bound to impose self-restraint in

---

28   Ibid., 212.
29   On Freud's resistance to nationalism and Zionism, see Jacqueline Rose, *The Last Resistance*, London and New York: Verso, 2007, 17–38.

the name of the preservation of life, opens the possibility of a democratization of critical judgment and critical thought that does not rely on the extremes of super-egoic self-flagellation to arrive at a moral position. Does he, in the end, offer a convincing response to the skeptical position that the destructive powers of humans are so profoundly inscribed in the life of the drives that no political arrangement can effectively check them? On the one hand, Freud argues that we must rally behind love, which builds and preserves social bonds, and behind identification, which builds and preserves sentiments of solidarity, over and against hate (or Thanatos), which tears at social bonds in wild and mindless ways. On the other hand, he has time and again underscored the fact that love and hate are equally constitutive dimensions of the drives, and that it is not possible to eliminate destructiveness simply by amplifying Eros. It is not only that we must sometimes *aggressively* defend our lives in order to preserve life (the aim of Eros); we also have to commit to living with those toward whom we maintain intense feelings of hostility and murderous impulse.

In his discussion of identification and melancholia, it is clear that all love relations contain ambivalence, pushed in two countervailing directions understood as the propulsions of love and hate. So, "love" names one pole in the oppositional relation of love and hate. But it also names the opposition itself, lived out as emotional ambivalence and its vacillating variations. One can say, "I love you and so do not hate you," but one can also say that love and hate are bound together, and this paradox is what we include under the name of "love." In the former formulation, love is unequivocal; in the latter formulation, love does not escape ambivalence. Is there something about the rhythm, however jarring, established between these two formulations that constitutes a broader concept of love for Freud?

There seem to be two consequences, then, of Freud's views on destructiveness and war that are opened up but not precisely pursued. The first is that a corrective to forms of accelerated nationalist sentiment is precisely ambivalence, the "tearing" at the social bond that follows from a mindful self-distancing from its exhilarations and hostilities—and from the restrictively nationalist framework. One might, at the same time, love a country and dissent from its nationalist fervor; that would activate ambivalence in the service of a critical reflection on the possibility of war and a refusal to partake in its excitations. The second consequence would be to rally hatred against war itself. Freud offers this indirectly, in his letter to Einstein, in his own rhetoric. For instance, he writes, "The basis for our common hatred of war . . . is that we cannot do otherwise than to hate it. Pacifists we are because our organic nature wills us thus to be."[30]

This is a sweeping and suspect claim, to be sure. So what is Freud doing when he writes in this way? On the one hand, he has told us that the death drive is an "unconquerable" dimension of our organic lives; on the other hand, there seems to be a drive toward life, or a vitalistic drive to live—one that seeks to overthrow the threat to life itself. Only one part of our organic nature wills us to be pacifists, the part that would value the sentiments of solidarity: those that seek to overthrow the forces of destruction and the anthropomorphic fascination of tyrannical power. So, he is effectively calling

---

30   Freud to Einstein, "Why War?," 214.

upon, or calling to, that part of our organic natures that could be pacificist if it were to gain power over destructive impulses, subordinating the latter to the aims of collective self-preservation.

Freud calls on organic nature to manifest its necessary pacifism, but this can only happen where the "growth of culture" has produced a resentment against war and the felt sense of its intolerable character. It is thus only an *educated* organic nature that discovers that war sensations are no longer thrilling, because only through an educated optic can any of us see—and imagine—the destruction of organic life that war implies, something that proves unbearable for humans to accept in light of their own organic life. On the one hand, it is organic life that makes us pacifists, since at least some part of us does not will our own destruction (when we are not under the dominant sway of the death drive). On the other hand, we only come to understand the consequences of the destruction of organic life through a cultural process that allows us to see and consider this destruction, and so to develop a revulsion against destruction itself. In the end, Freud hopes that another vicissitude of organic life will have the final say against the death drive, whose aim is the destruction of that very life, and that various forms of organic life will come to be understood as connected through relations of dependency that extend throughout the living world. In this way, his is a politics of and for the living organism, even if the organism is sometimes swayed by the circuitous or destructive path toward death. Hatred is never fully absent, but its negative power can become focused as an aggressive stance against war, one form of destruction pitted against another—a view that would be compatible, for instance, with an aggressive form of pacifism, what Einstein himself called "militant pacifism."[31]

Gandhi, too, seemed to be engaged in his own drive theory in a similar way when he remarked, "I have found that life persists in the midst of destruction and, therefore, there must be a higher law than that of destruction."[32] He relates this as well to "the law of love." Whatever form this "law" may take, it also seems to take form in the rhetorical appeal to the law, the petition to avert destruction. It may not rest upon a discoverable law; rather, it is, like the demands of organic nature, a political and ethical rhetoric that seeks to compel and persuade in the direction of nonviolence, precisely on those occasions where the full lure of violence is registered.

Freud's appeal to nonviolence operates, as well, in a psychic and social field where actions are pulled in countervailing directions. Whatever "law" imposes itself against violence is not a law that can be codified or applied. It structures the appeal itself, the address to the other, the ethical bond presupposed and enlivening through that appeal. Further, that does not mean that there is no place for destruction, in the sense of breaking with subordination or dismantling an unjust regime. The subject who is obedient

31 See Albert Einstein's interview with George Sylvester Viereck in January 1931, where he claims: "I am not only a pacifist, but a militant pacifist. I am willing to fight for peace. Nothing will end war unless the peoples themselves refuse to go to war. Every great cause is first championed by an aggressive minority." In *Einstein on Peace*, Otto Nathan and Heinz Norden, eds., Pickle Partners Publishing, 2017, 125.

32 Mahatma Gandhi, "My Faith in Nonviolence," in Arthur and Lila Weinberg, eds., *The Power of Nonviolence: Writings by Advocates of Peace*, Boston: Beacon Press, 2002, 45.

to a murderous form of power enacts that violence against itself, setting up that political power as the structure of the super-ego, an internalized form of violence. The limit point of the super-ego is the destruction of the ego and of the living organism itself (suicide or murder), but the form of aggression that Freud imagines, at the end of his correspondence with Einstein, is of a different order. When he remarks that the only hope for prevailing against the tyrant is the mobilization of mania (leveling plaint after plaint, until numerosity overwhelms sovereign power), he offers us a glimpse into those forms of insurrectionary solidarity that turn against authoritarian and tyrannical rule, as well as against forms of war that threaten the destruction of life itself. The hatred directed against war is perhaps like the mania that alone has the strength to free the subject from the tyrant; both break with nationalist and militarist forms of social belonging through turning one sense of the critical faculty against another. The critical faculty that becomes animated in the name of a democratization of dissent is one that opposes war and resists the intoxications of nationalism, turning against the leader who insists that obedience to a war-mongering authority is obligatory. In this way, Freud imagines the democratization of critical judgment based on sentiments of solidarity, one that turns against that life-threatening form of aggression, including its critical manifestation. Aggression and hatred both remain, for sure, but they are now directed against all that which undermines the prospect of expanding equality and which imperils the organic persistence of our interconnected lives. But nothing remains guaranteed, for the death drive appears, as well, to be part of organic life; so, if the organic turns out to be driven by the duality of life and death, that should hardly come as a total surprise. The struggle that constitutes us as political creatures is the one we continue, without a perfect conscious understanding, in the practices of life and death, despite our occasional admirably decisive efforts at vigilance.

Postscript: Rethinking Vulnerability, Violence, Resistance

We are living in a time of numerous atrocities and senseless death, to be sure, and so one of the enormous ethical and political questions becomes: What are the modes of representation that are available to us to apprehend this violence? Some would say that global and regional authorities have to identify vulnerable groups and offer them protection. And though I am not opposed to the proliferation of "vulnerability papers" that would allow more migrants to cross borders, I am wondering whether that particular formation of discourse and power gets to the heart of the problem. The criticism is now well known that the discourse of "vulnerable groups" reproduces paternalistic power and gives authority to regulatory agencies with interests and constraints of their own. At the same time, I am mindful that many advocates for vulnerability have sought to address this very issue in their empirical and theoretical work.[1]

---

1 See Martha Fineman's website foregrounding the scholarship of her research team at Emory University: "Vulnerability and the Human

What seems clear is that, as important as it is to revalue vulnerability and give place to care, neither vulnerability nor care can serve as the basis of a politics. I would surely like to be a better person and to strive to become that, in part by acknowledging my apparently profound and recurrent fallibility. But none of us should seek to be saints, if what that means is that we hoard all goodness for ourselves, expelling the flawed or destructive dimension of the human psyche to actors on the outside, those living in the region of the "not me," with whom we dis-identify. If, for instance, by an ethics or politics of "care" we mean that an ongoing and un-conflicted human disposition can and should give rise to a political framework for feminism, then we have entered into a bifurcated reality in which our own aggression is edited out of the picture or projected onto others. Similarly, it would be easy and efficient if we could establish vulnerability as the foundation for a new politics; but considered as a condition, it can neither be isolated from other terms, nor be the kind of phenomenon that can serve as a foundation. Is anyone vulnerable, for instance, without persisting in a vulnerable condition? Further, if we think about those who, in a condition of vulnerability, resist that very condition, how do we understand that duality?

The task, I would suggest, is not to rally as vulnerable creatures or to create a class of persons who identify primarily with vulnerability. In portraying people and communities who are subject to violence in systematic ways, do we do them justice, do we respect the dignity of their struggle, if we

Condition," Emory University official website, web.gs.emory.edu/vulnerability.

summarize them as "the vulnerable"? In the context of human rights work, the category of "vulnerable populations" includes those who require protection and care. Of course, it is crucial to bring into public awareness the situation of those who lack basic human requirements such as food and shelter, but also those whose freedom of mobility and rights to legal citizenship are denied, if not criminalized. Indeed, an increasingly large number of refugees have been abandoned by so many nation-states and transnational state formations, including, of course, the European Union. And the United Nations High Commissioner for Refugees estimates there are nearly 10 million stateless people now living in the world.[2] We also speak in such a way about the victims of feminicídio in Latin America (nearly 3,000 every year, with especially high rates in Honduras, Guatemala, Brazil, Argentina, Venezuela, and El Salvador), a term which includes everyone who is brutalized or killed by virtue of being feminized, including large numbers of trans women as well.[3] At the same time, the Ni Una Menos movement has mobilized over a million women across Latin America (and Spain and Italy) to protest *machista* violence by taking to the streets. Organizing women and trans communities, *travestis* as well, Ni Una Menos has entered schools, churches, and unions to connect with women across

---

2 United Nations High Commissioner for Refugees, *Statelessness around the World*, UNHCR official website, unhcr.org.

3 "Countries with the Highest Number of Murders of Trans and Gender-Diverse People in Latin America from January to September 2018," Trans Murder Monitoring, November 2018, statista.com/statistics/944650/number-trans-murders-latin-america-country. See also Chase Strangio, "Deadly Violence against Transgender People Is on the Rise. The Government Isn't Helping," ACLU, August 21, 2018, aclu.org.

economic classes and different regional communities to oppose the killing of women and trans people, but also the persistence of discrimination, battery, and systemic inequality.

Often the deaths from feminicídio are reported as sensationalist stories, after which there is a momentary shock. And then it happens again. There is horror, to be sure, but it is not always linked with an analysis and a mobilization that focuses collective rage. The systemic character of this violence is effaced when the men who commit such crimes are said to suffer personality disorders or singular pathological conditions. That same effacement happens when a death is considered to be "tragic," as if conflicting forces in the universe led to an unfortunate conclusion. In Costa Rica, sociologist Montserrat Sagot has argued that the violence against women not only brings into focus the systemic inequality between men and women throughout society, but manifests forms of terror that are part of the legacy of dictatorial power and military violence.[4] The impunity with which brutal murders are treated continues violent legacies where domination, terror, social vulnerability, and extermination were committed on a regular basis. In her view, it will not do to explain assassinations such as these through recourse to individual characteristics, pathology, or even masculine aggression. Rather, these acts of killing have to be understood in terms of the reproduction of a social structure. She claims, further, that they have to be described as an extreme form of sexist terrorism.[5]

---

4   Montserrat Sagot, "A rota crítica da violência intrafamiliar em países latino-americanos," in Stela Nazareth Meneghel, ed., *Rotas críticas: mulheres enfrentando a violência*, São Leopoldo: Editoria Usinos, 2007, 23–50.

5   See also Julia Estela Monárrez Fragoso, "Serial Sexual Femicide in Ciudad Juárez: 1993–2001," *Debate Femenista* 13:25, 2002.

For Sagot, killing is the most extreme form of domination, and other forms, including discrimination, harassment, and battery, have to be understood as on a continuum with feminicídio. This is not a causal argument, yet every form of domination signals this lethal conclusion as a potential. Sexual violence carries with it the threat of death, and too often, it makes good on that promise.

Feminicídio works, in part, through establishing a climate of fear in which any woman, including trans women, can be killed. And this fear is compounded among women of color and queers of color, especially in Brazil. Those who are living understand themselves as *still living*, living in spite of this ambient threat, and they endure, and breathe, within an atmosphere of potential harm. Women who live on in such a climate are to some degree terrorized by the prevalence and impunity of this killing practice. They are induced to subordinate to men in order to avoid that fate, which means that their experience of inequality and subordination is already linked to their status as "killable." "Subordinate or die" may seem like a hyperbolic imperative, but it is the message that many women know is addressed to them. This power to terrorize is too often backed up, supported, and strengthened by police and court systems that refuse to prosecute, that do not recognize the criminal character of the action. Sometimes violence is inflicted again on women who dare to make a legal complaint, punishing that manifestation of courage and persistence.

The killing is the obviously violent act in this scenario, but it would not reproduce with such great speed and intensity if it were not for those who dismiss the crime, blame the victim, or pathologize the killer in the spirit of exoneration.

Indeed, impunity is all too often built into the legal structure (which is one reason local authorities resist the intervention of the Inter-American Court of Human Rights), meaning that the refusal to receive the report, the threats against those who make the report, and the failure to recognize the crime all perpetuate this violence and give license to murder. In such a case, we have to locate violence in the act, but also in the foreshadowing exhibited by the social domination of women—and of the feminized. Violence occurs in the series of legal refusals and failures to recognize it as such: no report means no crime, no punishment, and no reparation.

If feminicídio is understood as producing sexual terror, then these feminist and trans struggles are not only bound together (as they should be) but linked to struggles of queer people, of all those fighting homophobia, and of people of color who are disproportionately the target of violence or abandonment. If sexual terror is related not only to domination, but to extermination, then sexual violence constitutes a dense site for complex histories of oppression as well as of resistance struggles. As individual and awful as each of these losses surely is, they belong to a social structure that has deemed women *ungrievable*. The act of violence enacts the social structure, and the social structure exceeds each of the acts of violence by which it is manifested and reproduced. These are losses that should not have happened, that should never happen again: *Ni Una Menos*.

My example does not do justice to the historical specificity of these acts of violence, but perhaps it introduces a set of questions that can be helpful as we seek to understand murder upon murder as something other than isolated and terrible acts. The ethical and epistemological demand to create a global picture and account of this reality would have to include the killings that take place in US prisons and streets, which are the responsibility of the police who often make law on the spot. The right-wing populist embrace of new authoritarianisms, new security rationales, and new powers for security forces, police, and military (and the particular merging of all three that seems increasingly to monitor public space) supposes that such lethal institutions are necessary to "protect" the "people" from violence; and yet, such justifications only expand police powers and subject those on the margins to ever more intense carceral strategies of containment and restriction.

Is there, then, a way to name and counter forms of necropolitical targeting such as these without producing a class of victims that denies women, queers, trans people, and people of color (more generally) their networks, their theory and analysis, their solidarities, and their power to wage an effective opposition? The police seek to "protect" the people against violence and expand their carceral powers in the name of that protection. Are we unwittingly doing something similar when we speak about "vulnerable populations," and the task thus becomes to relieve them of such vulnerability? That task is undertaken by an organization or agency that seeks to provide that relief. Relief from precarity is good, but does that approach grasp and oppose the structural forms of violence and the economics that dispose populations to unlivable precarity? Why is it that "we" do not forfeit the paternalistic option, as it were, in order to join solidarity networks, opposing such forms of social domination and violence, with those who are at once vulnerable *and* struggling? Once "the vulnerable" are constituted as such, are they understood to still maintain and exercise their own power? Or has all the power vanished from the situation of the vulnerable, resurfacing as the power of paternalistic care now obligated to intervene?

What if the situation of those deemed vulnerable is, in fact, a constellation of vulnerability, rage, persistence, and resistance that emerges under these same historical conditions? It would be equally unwise to *extract* vulnerability from this constellation; indeed, vulnerability traverses and conditions social relations, and without that insight we stand little chance of realizing the sort of substantive equality that is desired. Vulnerability ought not to be identified exclusively with passivity; it makes sense only in light of an embodied set of social relations, including practices of resistance. A view of vulnerability as part of embodied social relations and actions can help us understand how and why forms of resistance emerge as they do. Although domination is not always followed by resistance, if our frameworks of power fail to grasp how vulnerability and resistance can work together, we risk being unable to identify those sites of resistance that are opened up by vulnerability.

That said, it is clear that the organized character of deprivation and death that has taken place along the extended borders of Europe is enormous, and that the resistance of migrants and their allies is crucial, if only episodic. Approximately 5,400 people died trying to cross the Mediterranean in 2017–18 alone, and these include the large numbers of Kurdish people seeking to migrate over the sea.[6] The Syrian Network for Human Rights reports that

---

6   International Organization for Migration, "Mediterranean Migrant

on the eighth anniversary of the uprising in March 2019, the death toll for civilians had reached 221,161.[7] There are many examples on which we could draw, in addition to feminicídio, to raise the question of how we come to name and understand the organization of populations primed for dispossession and death; they would include the brutal treatment of Syrians and Kurds amassed on the border of Turkey, and anti-Muslim racism in Europe and the United States, as well as its convergence with anti-migrant and anti-black racism that creates the notion of disposable peoples—those who are considered on the cusp of death or already dead.

At the same time, those who have lost infrastructural support have developed networks, communicated timetables, and sought to understand and use international maritime laws in the Mediterranean to their advantage in order to move across borders—to plot a route and to connect with communities that can provide support of one kind or another, such as squatting in vacated hotels with accommodating anarchists. Those amassed along the borders of Europe are not precisely what political philosopher Giorgio Agamben referred to as "bare life"—that is to say, we do not recognize their suffering by further depriving them of all capacity. Rather, they are, for the most part, in a terrible situation: improvising forms of sociality, using cell phones,

---

Arrivals Reach 113,145 in 2018; Deaths Reach 2,242," International Organization for Migration official website, 2018, iom.int; "Mediterranean: Deaths by Route," Missing Migrants Project, missingmigrants.iom.int, accessed May 15, 2019.

7   Syrian Network for Human Rights, "Eight Years Since the Start of the Popular Uprising in Syria, Terrible Violations Continue," Syrian Network for Human Rights official website, 2019, sn4hr.org.

plotting and taking action when it is possible, drawing maps, learning languages, though in so many instances those activities are not always possible. Even as agency is blocked at every turn, there still remain ways of resisting that very blockage, ways of entering the force field of violence to stop its continuation. When they do make the demand for papers, for movement, for entry, they are not precisely overcoming their vulnerability—they are *demonstrating it*, and *demonstrating with it*. What happens is not the miraculous or heroic transformation of vulnerability into strength, but the articulation of a demand that only a supported life can persist *as a life*. Sometimes the demand is made with the body, through showing up in a place where one is exposed to police power, and refusing to move. The cell phone image of the petitioner makes the virtual case for the actual life, and it shows how the life depends upon its virtual circulation. The body can only assert "this is a life" if the conditions of assertion can be established, that is, through its emphatic and public indexical demonstration.

Consider, for example, the German newspaper *Daily Resistance*, published in Farsi, Arabic, Turkish, German, French, and English, which contains articles by refugees who have formulated a set of political demands, including the abolition of all refugee camps, the end of the German policy of *Residenzpflicht* (which limits the freedom of movement of refugees within narrow boundaries), a halt to all deportations, and allowances for refugees to work and study.[8] In 2012, several refugees in the city of Würzburg stitched their

8 See my "Vulnerability and Resistance," *Profession*, March 2014, profession.mla.org.

mouths shut, protesting against the fact that the government had refused to respond to them. That gesture has been repeated in several sites, most recently by Iranian migrants in Calais, France, in March of 2017, before the destruction and evacuation of their camp. Their view, widely shared, is that without a political response, the refugees remain voiceless, since a voice that is not heard is not registered, and so is not a political voice. Of course, they did not put their claim in this propositional form. But they made the point through a readable and visible gesture that muted the voice as the sign and substance of their demand. The image of the stitched lips shows that the demand cannot be voiced and so makes its own voiceless demand. It displays its voicelessness in a visual image in order to make a point about the political limits imposed on audibility. In some ways, we see again a form of theatrical politics that asserts their power and, at the same time, the limits imposed on that power.

Another example from Turkey is the "standing man" in Taksim Square in June of 2013 who was part of the protest movements against the Erdoğan government, including against its policies of privatization and its authoritarianism. The standing man was a performance artist, Erdem Gündüz, who obeyed the state's edict, delivered immediately after the mass protests, not to assemble and not to speak with others in assembly—an edict by Erdoğan that sought to undermine the most basic premises of democracy: freedom of movement, of assembly, and of speech. So, one man stood, and stood at the mandated distance from another person, who in turn stood at the mandated distance from another. Legally, they did not constitute an assembly, and no one was speaking or moving. What they did was to perform compliance perfectly, hundreds of them, filling the square at the proper distance from one another. They effectively demonstrated the ban under which they were living, submitting to it at the same time that they displayed it for the cameras, which could not be fully banned. Demonstration had at least two meanings: the ban was shown, incorporated, enacted bodily—the ban became a script—but the ban was also opposed, demonstrated against. That demonstration was elaborated in and by the visual field opened up by cell phone cameras, those forms of technology that eluded the interdiction on speech and movement. The performance thus both submitted to and defied the interdiction, in and through the same action. It shows the knotted position of the subjugated subject by at once exposing and opposing its own subjugation.

In such cases, the living character of the subjugated is also brought to the fore: This will not be a life sequestered in its subjugation, deprived of appearance and speech in the public sphere; this will be a *living* life, and that redoubling means that it is not yet extinguished, and that it continues to make a claim and demand on behalf of its own living character. The bodies that say, "I will not disappear so easily," or, "My disappearance will leave a vibrant trace from which resistance will grow," are effectively asserting their grievability within the public and media sphere. In exposing their bodies in the context of demonstration, they let it be known which bodies are at risk of detention, deportation, or death. For embodied performance brings that specific historical exposure to violence to the fore; it makes the wager and the demand with its own performative and embodied persistence. Note that it is not the immediacy of the body that makes this demand, but rather the body as socially regulated and abandoned, the body as persisting and resisting that very regulation, asserting its existence within readable terms.[9] It acts as its own *deixis,* a pointing to, or enacting of, the body that implies its situation: *this* body, *these* bodies; *these* are the ones exposed to violence, resisting disappearance. These bodies exist still, which is to say that they persist under conditions in which their very power to persist is systematically undermined.

This persistence is not a matter of heroic individualism, or one of digging deep into unknown personal resources. The body, in its persistence, is neither an expression of the individual nor a collective will. For if we accept that part of what a body is (and this is for the moment an ontological claim) occurs in its dependency on other bodies—on living processes of which it is a part, on networks of support to which it also contributes—then we are suggesting that it is not altogether right to conceive of individual bodies as completely distinct from one another; and neither would it be right to think of them as fully merged, without distinction. Without conceptualizing the political meaning of the human body in the context of those institutions, practices, and relations in which it lives and thrives, we fail to make the best possible case for why murder is unacceptable, abandonment has to be opposed, and precarity has to be alleviated. It is not just that this or that body is bound up in a network of relations, but that the boundary both contains and relates; the body, perhaps precisely by virtue of its boundaries, is differentiated from and exposed to a material and social

9 See Lauren Wilcox, *Bodies of Violence: Theorizing Embodied Subjects in International Relations*, Oxford, UK: Oxford University Press, 2015.

world that makes its own life and action possible. When the infrastructural conditions of life are imperiled, so too is life, since life requires infrastructure, not simply as an external support, but as an immanent feature of life itself. This is a materialist point we deny only at our own peril.

Critical social theory has not always taken into account the way in which life and death are presupposed by the ways we think about social relations. For it is one thing to say that life and death are both socially organized, and that we can describe social forms of living and dying. That is important work, to be sure. But if we do not consider what we mean by "the social" in such discussions, we may fail to see how the threat of death and the promise of life are constitutive features of those relations that we call "social." So, in some ways, our habits of constructivism have to change in order to grasp the issues of life and death at issue here: those of bodily persistence, of the fact that there are always conditions for bodily persistence. Where those conditions for bodily persistence are not actualized, persistence is threatened.

If there is a right to persist, it would not be one that individuals maintain at the expense of their social condition. Individualism fails to capture the condition of vulnerability, exposure, even dependency, that is presupposed by the right itself, and that corresponds, I would suggest, to a body whose boundaries are themselves fraught and excitable social relations. Whether a body that falters and falls is caught by networks of support, or whether a moving body has its way paved without obstruction, depends on whether a world has been built for both its gravity and mobility— and whether that world can stay built. The skin is, from the start, a way of being exposed to the elements, but that exposure always takes a social form. And what is done about that exposure is already a socially organized relation: a relation to shelter, to adequate clothing, to health services. If we seek to find what is most essential about the body by reducing it to its bare elements or even to its bare life, we find that right there at the level of its most basic requirements, the social world is already structuring the scene. Thus, the basic questions of mobility, expression, warmth, and health implicate that body in a social world where pathways are differentially paved, are open or closed; and where modes of clothing and types of shelter are more or less available, affordable, or provisional. The body is invariably defined by the social relations that bear upon its persistence, sustenance, and thriving.

The thriving that is bound up with human life is connected to the thriving of non-human creatures; human and non-human life are also related by virtue of the living processes they are, they share and they require, raising all kinds of questions about stewardship that deserve full attention from scholars and intellectuals across all fields. The political concept of self-preservation, often used in the defense of violent action, does not consider that the preservation of the self requires the preservation of the earth, and that we are not "in" the global environment as self-subsisting beings, but subsist only as long as the planet does. What is true for humans is true for all living creatures who require non-toxic soil and clean water for the continuation of life.[10] If any of

---

10   Donna Haraway, *The Companion Species Manifesto*, Chicago: Prickly Paradigm, 2003; and *When Species Meet*, Minneapolis: University of Minnesota Press, 2007.

us are to survive, to flourish, even to attempt to lead a good life, it will be a life lived with others—a live that is no life without those others. I will not lose this "I" who I am under such conditions; rather, if I am lucky, and the world is right, whoever I am will be steadily sustained and transformed by my connections with others, the forms of contact by which I am altered and sustained.

The dyadic relation tells only part of the story—the part that can be exemplified by the encounter. This "I" requires a "you" in order to survive and to flourish. Yet, both the "I" and the "you" require a sustaining world. These social relations can serve as a ground for thinking about the broader global obligations of nonviolence we bear toward one another: I cannot live without living together with some set of people, and it is invariable that the potential for destruction dwells precisely in that necessary relationship. That one group cannot live without living together with another such group means that one's own life is already in some sense the life of the other. And then there are the growing numbers of those who no longer belong to a nation, or who have lost their territorial grounding, seen it bombed or stolen; those who have been expelled from whatever category tenuously held them within its terms, carrying forth unbearable losses into a new language they have just begun to speak, summarily clustered as the "stateless" or the "migrant" or the "indigenous."

The ties that potentially bind us across zones of geopolitical violence can be unknowing and frail, freighted with paternalism and power, but they can be strengthened through transversal forms of solidarity that dispute the primacy and necessity of violence. The sentiments of solidarity that persist are those that accept the transversal character of our alliances, the perpetual demand for translation as well as the epistemic limits that mark its failures, including its appropriations and effacements. To avow vulnerability not as an attribute of the subject, but as a feature of social relations, does not imply vulnerability as an identity, a category, or a ground for political action. Rather, persistence in a condition of vulnerability proves to be its own kind of strength, distinguished from one that champions strength as the achievement of invulnerability. That condition of mastery replicates the forms of domination to be opposed, devaluing those forms of susceptibility and contagion that yield solidarity and transformational alliances.

Similarly, the prejudice against nonviolence as passive and useless implicitly depends upon a gendered division of attributes by which masculinity stands for activity, and femininity for passivity. No transvaluation of those values will defeat the falsehood of that binary opposition. Indeed, the power of nonviolence, its force, is found in the modes of resistance to a form of violence that regularly hides its true name. Nonviolence exposes the ruse by which state violence defends itself against black and brown people, queer people, the migrant, the homeless, the dissenters—as if they were, taken together, so many vessels of destruction who must, for "security reasons," be detained, incarcerated, or expelled. The "soul force" that Gandhi had in mind was never fully separable from an embodied stance, a way of living in the body and of persisting, precisely under conditions that attack the very conditions of persistence. Sometimes continuing to exist in the vexation of social relations is the ultimate defeat of violent power.

To link a practice of nonviolence with a force or strength that is distinguished from destructive violence, one that is manifest in solidarity alliances of resistance and persistence, is to refute the characterization of nonviolence as a weak and useless passivity. Refusal is not the same as doing nothing. The hunger striker refuses to reproduce the prisoner's body, indicting the carceral powers that are already attacking the existence of the incarcerated. The strike may not seem like an "action," but it asserts its power by withdrawing labor that is essential to the continuation of a capitalist form of exploitation. Civil disobedience may seem like a simple "opting out," but it makes public a judgment that a legal system is not just. It requires the exercise of an extra-legal judgment. To breach the fence or the wall that is designed to keep people out is precisely to exercise an extra-legal claim to freedom, one that the existing legal regime is failing to provide for within its own terms. To boycott a regime that continues colonial rule, intensifying dispossession, displacement, and disenfranchisement for an entire population, is to assert the injustice of the regime, to refuse to reproduce its criminality as normal.

For nonviolence to escape the war logics that distinguish between lives worth preserving and lives considered dispensable, it must become part of a politics of equality. Thus, an intervention in the sphere of appearance—the media and all the contemporary permutations of the public sphere—is required to make every life grievable, that is, worthy of its own living, deserving of its own life. To demand that every life be grievable is another way of saying that all lives ought to be able to persist in their living without being subject to violence, systemic abandonment, or military obliteration.

To counter the scheme of lethal phantasmagoria that so often justifies police violence against black and brown communities, military violence against migrants, and state violence against dissidents, a new imaginary is required— an egalitarian imaginary that apprehends the interdependency of lives. Unrealistic and useless, yes, but it is possibly a way of bringing another reality into being that does not rely on instrumental logics and the racial phantasmagoria that reproduces state violence. The "unrealism" of such an imaginary is its strength. It is not just that in such a world, each life would deserve to be treated as the other's equal, or that each would have an equal right to live and to flourish—although certainly both of those possibilities are to be affirmed. A further step is required: "each" is, from the start, given over to another, social, dependent, but without the proper resources to know whether this dependency that is required for life is exploitation or love.

We do not have to love one another to engage in meaningful solidarity. The emergence of a critical faculty, of critique itself, is bound up with the vexed and precious relationship of solidarity, where our "sentiments" navigate the ambivalence by which they are constituted. We can always fall apart, which is why we struggle to stay together. Only then do we stand a chance of persisting in a critical commons: when nonviolence becomes the desire for the other's desire to live, a way of saying, "You are grievable; the loss of you is intolerable; and I want you to live; I want you to want to live, so take my desire as your desire, for yours is already mine." The "I" is not you, yet it remains unthinkable without the "you"—worldless, unsustainable. So, whether we are caught up in rage or love—rageful love, militant pacifism, aggressive nonviolence, radical persistence—let us hope that we live that bind in ways that let us live with the living, mindful of the dead, demonstrating persistence in the midst of grief and rage, the rocky and vexed trajectory of collective action in the shadow of fatality.

Index